Letters from Lost Thyme

TWO DECADES OF LETTERS
FROM JOHN JOSEPH
TO PATRICIA LARSEN

introduction by EDWARD ALBEE

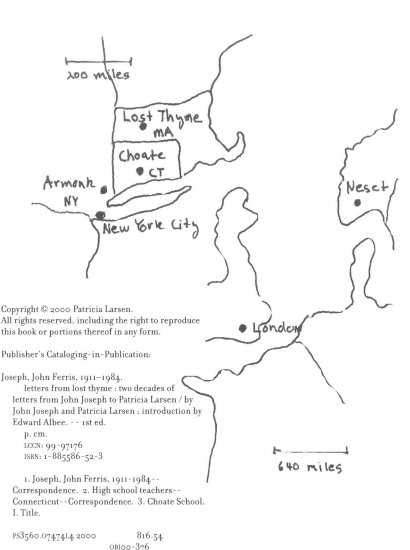

Publisher's Cataloging-in-Publication:

Joseph, John Ferris, 1911–1984.
    letters from lost thyme : two decades of
    letters from John Joseph to Patricia Larsen / by
    John Joseph and Patricia Larsen ; introduction by
    Edward Albee. -- 1st ed.
        p. cm.
        LCCN: 99-97176
        ISBN: 1-885586-52-3

    1. Joseph, John Ferris, 1911-1984--
Correspondence. 2. High school teachers--
Connecticut--Correspondence. 3. Choate School.
I. Title.

PS3560.07474L4 2000   816.54
                    QBI00-376

Printed in Canada.

Front cover art and copyright page map: Peik Larsen
Back cover and inside cover art: Patricia Larsen
Text and cover design and composition: Anne Galperin

Editor's Introduction

I have derived enormous enjoyment sorting through the letters John Joseph of Lost Thyme wrote to Patricia Larsen over the course of two decades. Because John Joseph loved to write about the things in which he delighted, and he wrote well, I've been able to share his relish for such sensory and intellectual pleasures as gardening, cooking, eating, reading, and outings with friends. *These* were his pleasures in life, and his enthusiasm is contagious.

Craig Metzler, John Joseph's close companion in his later years and the friend who was with him when he uttered his last words, "Catch me, I'm falling," generously gave of his time and his memories. Jeannette Watson (publisher of Books & Co.) and I spent a lovely summer day with Craig during which he took us to see Lost Thyme, which had begun to deteriorate, but is now in the process of being lovingly restored by its new owners. Craig also showed us the commemorative video John Joseph's student Monty Hunter made in 1982 entitled "Mr. Joseph at Lost Thyme." In the video, Mr. Hunter closely questioned John Joseph about his philosophy of life and John Joseph responded, as was his wont, with eloquence and charm. With Mr. Hunter's gracious permission, I have incorporated portions of John Joseph's remarks wherever I felt they added an extra dimension to the subject at hand.

In his letter of 11 August 1980, John Joseph remarked on Mrs. Larsen's enthusiastic discovery of the published volumes of the correspondence between George Lyttelton and Rupert Hart-Davis. "I have ever been one to delve into the letters of others," he wrote. "Nosey, in short; but of how many delightful hours should I have deprived myself all these years were I not nosey." I hope that this edition of John Joseph's letters will offer you, as well, "many delightful hours."

❦ Hélène Golay, April 2000

Some Thoughts on Civilization

EDWARD ALBEE

I never had a class with John Joseph while I was at Choate, but he did let me into his life. I can't recall when he first invited me to his rooms, but I do recall being there, marvelling that someone had reads so much, knew so much—about food, about literature, about music, about....well, about civilization, and that that some- one was willing to share it all with me, an eager, unformed young man who had been touched by the arts but was only at the gates to the wonders.

People like John Joseph—what an odd phrase! There are no people like John Joseph. People approaching John Joseph (there!

that's better!) can happen to kids at a school like Choate. I was lucky; I ran into three or four teachers who instructed me outside of class as well as in—about the visual arts, about poetry, about music—but had there been only John that would have been enough.

"Look," these teachers say, taking you by the mental hand, "there is this thing called civilization. You are nothing if you don't understand it. Learn; learn eagerly!"

And some of us do and are eternally grateful.

I would see John occasionally after I left Choate, and he treated me no differently than when I was a student. Doubtless I still was!

It is interesting to me that John was only seventeen years my senior, that he was thirty five when I sat figuratively at his knee when I was eighteen. He always seemed so much older. I think he was always middle-aged.

What did I admire most about him—aside from all I have mentioned? Well, his privacy, probably. He shared much, and his enthusiasms were multifold and passionate, but there was a private man there, a wounded man, I think, a shy and solitary figure, and I admired him too much to probe.

These letters tell us much about John Joseph—his erudition, his broad range of enthusiasms, his love of that which deserved love, and his existential sense of life; and while there are glimpses of a dark and bitter side I am most moved by his love of being alive.

And as he died, falling, saying "Catch me! I'm falling!" O how I wish I could have been there to catch him as he fell, held him as he lay on the earth he loved so well.

❦ November 1999

JOHN JOSEPH AT HOME AT LOST THYME.

I THINK I'M THE ONLY 18TH CENTURY MAN IN THE WORLD
LEFT, BECAUSE EVERY MORNING OF MY LIFE I SPEND ABOUT AN
HOUR OR TWO WRITING LETTERS. WRITING LETTERS IS A
GREAT DELIGHT TO ME AND I WRITE BRIEF LETTERS: I DO NOT
WRITE LONG, COMPLICATED LETTERS. I NEVER USE MORE THAN
ONE PIECE OF PAPER, BECAUSE I BELIEVE YOU CAN SAY IT ALL
ON ONE PAGE SUCCINCTLY, AND CLEARLY, AND COMPLETELY.

FROM *Mr. Joseph at Lost Thyme*, 1982

I met John Joseph at the Choate School in the autumn of 1967 through Per, the third of my husband Harry's and my four sons who went to Choate. The son of Lebanese parents who had immigrated to Boston, John Joseph attended the prestigious Boston Latin Public School and graduated with two degrees from Harvard University. In 1944 he joined the faculty of Choate where he taught etymology, Latin, Greek, and Sixth Form Honors English. During Per's time at Choate, John Joseph also started a course in forestry and would take Per and others for long hikes in the woods around Choate.

By the time I got to know John Joseph (he was always referred to as John Joseph), his hair was graying and he was going bald. His dark eyes were prominent and, when he was about to utter some bit of wisdom or tell a story, he would roll them up under his lids until they almost disappeared, and then open his mouth wide and lick his lips with the tip of his tongue. On his large nose he wore heavy-rimmed glasses which, when he wasn't reading, he pushed onto the top of his head. He smoked constantly, both cigarettes and a pipe. His outfit of old trousers with a sweater under a well-worn tweed coat and loose kerchief, tied in a debonair fashion around his neck, never varied.

Often on weekends, the slightly disheveled John Joseph, somewhat hunched and sporting his shapeless duck hat, could be seen with a cane striding purposely away from the playing fields of Choate to walk in precious solitude in the surrounding woods.

Choate was located in Wallingford, Connecticut, an easy drive from where we lived in Armonk. The students roomed in dormitories or in one of the small old farm houses situated around the campus. The Gables, where John Joseph was House Master, was one of these. It was a dilapidated building which housed 12 boys, including Per. His small living room was filled with books which were stacked on the floor, on the tables, the foot stools, the chairs and the sofa. The walls were hung frame to frame with prints, including some Piranesi and Daumiers. There was always a bowl of flowers beside the sherry decanter along with the unmatched glasses he would find on his many antique prowls.

John Joseph loved good food and was an excellent cook. He could produce a wonderful meal without seeming to leave his guests or interrupt his flow of conversation. Meals were served on delightful, unmatched china and glasses. The stove at the Gables, from which so many superb creations would appear, was a veritable antique with all the dials long since gone. The oven door had to be propped open with a large stone.

Lost Thyme was John Joseph's summer home in Shelbourne, Massachusetts, and later his retirement home when he left Choate after 33 years of teaching. It was a typical New England clapboard with a large bed of thyme in the front. In a picture I have of John Joseph taken at this retreat, he is characteristically leaning back in his chair—and sitting deeply, as the seat has apparently lost its springs—in a living room only slightly larger than that at the Gables. As at the Gables, the room speaks of the professorial disarray of a man with better things to do than keep house. In the photograph depicting his disorder, there's a round table, tilted slightly to the right, on which are strewn papers and books and a picture of Virginia Woolf resting against a silver candle stick. The pictures on the wall behind it and the lampshade on a small table next to it are askew, as is almost everything in the room, including a pair of desert boots next to John Joseph's chair. On the ottoman to his right is a stack of books and journals, and on the high table to his left are more books and leaning pictures. Outside the house was an overgrown field, a seemingly conscious travesty of an English manor, with no cows and deer grazing, and no English garden.

John Joseph was a great raconteur and a witty conversationalist, but it was his intense interest in people that made him such a magnet for so many boys who felt that here was a man whom they could admire, in whom they could confide, and who would treat their problems seriously and give them wise advice. He had a multitude of friends of all ages and both sexes, but he liked to see them singly or in small groups so that they could have his undivided attention.

Per, and then Leif (our fourth son), often had a difficult time adjusting to some of the mores of Choate, which they thought were unreasonable or unjust. I became apprehensive about opening report cards that would usually be filled with gloom and doom indicating that I had raised two nonconformists with anti-social tendencies who were being "less than Choate." It was John Joseph who reached out with his humanity. Not for him to censure long hair, slovenly clothes, and sloppy attitudes: he was there to teach.

I was to receive over 130 letters from J.J. over the next 17 years. This collection represents a portion of his half of our correspondence, as he burned all the letters from me (and others, as well). The first letter I received from John Joseph was to thank me for lending him Emerson's English Traits.

Très chère madame,

At last a chance to write to thank you for the Emerson. You will not believe it (for it is fashionable to believe that *no one* reads Emerson), but I delighted in every page of the book. I was particularly enchanted with the chapter on Stonehenge, one of my favorite spots on earth: and I had not known of Emerson's visit to the place with Carlyle. D'you know the essay? If you don't, delights await you. Concurrently with the Emerson I read Trollope's *Can You Forgive Her?* If you have not already met Lady Glenora and her husband Plantagenet Palisser, lucky you: more delights ahead. And, as I do every Christmas holiday, I revisited my friends Anna Karenina and Levin and all that delicious warm-hearted world of Tolstoy's great novel.

I read the Emerson, along with a small pile of favorites, in the warmth and serenity of the room I enjoyed at the house of friends in Southampton, the woods and the frozen bay outside my windows. I also walked copiously; dined well; wined elegantly; met and chatted with live, stimulating, unpedantic human beings from the outside world.

Your heir (Per) tea'd with me last Saturday and informed me that with you all went well. Good.

Yours, etc.
John Joseph

❦

Our friendship was cemented by my bringing to Choate a dinner for him and another master, Richard Hunter, a good friend of John Joseph's. I

*chose a "Poulet aux Quarante Gousse d'Ail" and "Orange Glacées"
from Julia Child's* Mastering the Art of French Cooking.

Très chère madame,

For the forty aromatic cloves, for the delightfully unostentatious little wines, for the dessert which looked as though the Hesperides devised it, for your wit, your warmth, and your intelligence—much thanks. Hunter and I are fortunate. Last night was pure 18th century, down to the fat spluttering altar candles that illuminated that segment of Hunter's flat where we dined. The care and devotion that went into peeling forty cloves of garlic, into julienning the vegetables and the orange peel, into planning and fulfilling the whole exquisite *repas*—these are the care and the devotion which one only too seldom, alas, encounters in these turbulent and chaotic times. He who encounters it now and then is a fortunate creature. Ergo, I am fortunate. And I am grateful. And so this puny effort at conveying, inadequately, I fear, my thanks. What is delicious is Per is aware of all this, delights in it, is proud of it, proud and grateful. It is a mark of a really wise child that he is aware of good fortune when it is his, aware and properly grateful. And Per is that. How nice to be so young and so sage. And so, at the risk of seeming tautological, *merci mille fois.*

Yours, etc.

John Joseph

❦ ❧

John Joseph spent his summers in Shelburne, Massachusetts, at his cottage called Lost Thyme. My husband, Harry, and I spent our summers in Norway where we had a 200-year old farm called Neset, on Totak Lake in Rauland. I first saw Neset on a bitterly cold day in June, 1954. I was sitting morosely on a wooden bench in the one-room farm house which housed two old built-in beds where the owners, Anna and Harold Neset, slept. Outside, the courtyard was mushy with rain. In its middle stood the pole for electricity with sagging lines. On one side were tumbled-down outbuildings built of grey logs with grass roofs that had turned to moss through neglect. As soon as the owner, Harold Neset, could be found, Harry was going to sign the bill of sale and we would become the owners of Neset Farm. Harry's good friend Esben Poulson, an architect, kept telling me that the farm had immense possibilities and that the view of Totak and the mountains across the lake and the foreground fields descending to a cove with a spit of land was superb, but that had no effect on my sullenness.

Eight months later when we returned, I walked into a Norwegian fairy tale and immediately fell in love with the place. The outbuildings with new turf roofs had been jacked up, the barn, the cow stable, and the goat house had all been repaired, and the telephone pole and wires had vanished. Two centuries of dirt and smoke had been washed from the old beds and the ceiling-high cupboard to disclose a "farmer's red" background and white panels, rose painted with free-flowing motifs and flowers. Throughout, Esben had thought of everything: curtains of hand-woven material, runners on the scrubbed white pine floors, antique tables, and benches. He had even left a freshly fished trout for dinner. Neset was a miracle!

LOST THYME
15 AUGUST 69

Très chère madame,

Here I am in utter solitude up in the hills but not really solitude, since an infinitude of birds, of insects, and of secret prowling little beasts are outside my door. My brook is deep and clear: and the vegetation everywhere is positively Amazonian, thanks to the tropically wet summer we have had. I have been working in brief spurts, have been reading (and rereading Gilbert White—d'you know him?), and taking prowls in the woods and on the mowings.

Yesterday I was plunged into an abysm of gloom for news reached me of the death, via an automobile crash, of one of the most devoted students I have known. Ironically, he dropped in on me at the Gables seven days ago to tell me that he had at last found serenity and joy. I never saw him look better, or sound more fulfilled. When I tried to persuade him to defer his return to Kentucky a day or two in order that he might come up here with me (for he'd been here and loved the woods), he said, regretfully, that he had to hurry home. And in hurrying home he was killed. His death has blackened the summer. And I do not see how parents survive such grim blows of fate, and to cap the ironies, as I was sorting papers this morning, I found an old letter from him in which he'd expressed hope to come up here again to walk the woods and to sit by the fire. My consolation is this: he was a *metaphysical* sort of a boy, eternally seeking the meaning behind meanings—the meaning of a cloud, of a wildflower, of a splash of sunlight, of a line of poetry. Mystical is the word for him: and now he is forever behind the purely physical. Poor dear chap, I hope he has the answers. It consoles me enormously that he has: and that in a simple unmysterious way his presence will always be felt up here in these woods and by the stream which once he dammed. (The dam still holds!)

Yours,
John Joseph

❦-❧

Although letters were sometimes infrequent, they were always spontaneous. This one concerning Leif, our youngest son, beautifully expresses the affectionate regard John Joseph felt for his students.

THURSDAY

4 JUNE 70

Très chère madame,

With you I must share a delightful gem. I was reading, yesterday afternoon, Leif's Examination in Philology. When I came to the little essay which he was required to write ("The Vitality of Slang"), I was absolutely, as you will be, enchanted by the flow of his prose and by the climax to which he constructs his thinking. Heed, O heed, his words: "Slang is always potent, especially in swearing, where its connotation cause it to either crack out or make one grit his teeth. For instance, when one gets his exam, he will open it up and look at the first problem and say, under his breath, *shhhhhit.* This has got to be the best phonetic sounding word for his feelings." I laughed until I realized that the boys outside my room must think me a madman. And now I share the gem with you. It is rich, no?

Yours, etc.
John Joseph

❦-❧

I'VE ALWAYS WANTED TO BE A TEACHER, AND, TOUCH WOOD, I'VE NEVER REGRETTED A DAY THAT I SPENT AT TEACHING. AND YOU ASK WHAT PART I LIKE THE BEST, I LIKE THE CLASSROOM. I LOVE THE SMELL OF CHALK. I LOVE DEMON-STRATING AT THE BLACKBOARD, I LOVE ANSWERING QUES-TIONS, AND MY PROUDEST BOAST IS THAT I THINK—I CAN SAY THIS WITHOUT ANY FEAR OF CONTRADICTION—NO ONE EVER FELL ASLEEP IN ONE OF MY CLASSROOMS. NO ONE EVER FELL ASLEEP.

Around this time John Joseph's friend Richard Hunter married Elizabeth Gray, a widow and the mother of two Choate boys. Gray's husband, an executive of the Reynolds Tobacco Company, had died of lung cancer leaving her a very rich widow.

LOST THYME
15 JUNE 70
{ TO ARMONK }
Très chère madame,

I have just come in from a spell of gardening: and without wasting a moment, I have come to my writing-table to give you a few lines. For this time there is news to impart, social notes from all over, as *The New Yorker* would phrase it. I refer, as you have guessed, to the Hunter-Gray bridals, which were quite some-thing. The few days I spent in North Carolina were like a sudden exhilarating dip into the 18th century: grand style, large and love-ly houses, incredible gardens (the boxwood would bring you to ecstasy), and swarms, perfect swarms of servants. I daresay it is the last-mentioned detail which makes the difference, which lends the last legitimate, indisputable 18th century touch. There were pre- and post-bridal festivities: most of them dinner—or luncheon—parties. And, damn it all, these Southerners know how to ooze with grace and charm and wit. (They also keep alive the fine art of gastronomy.)

The ceremony took place at her eldest son's house, a quiet, extremely dignified and somehow intensely religious service, with the Bishop of North Carolina officiating. Richard handled himself rather well, considering the solemnity of the occasion. She was absolutely stunning and looked young enough to be Richard's daughter. (He will have to thin out: he's lamentably fat.) I added spice to the proceedings by handing out to the Press an accumulation of whopping lies, all of which were scrupulously published in the local newsheet. Did you know, for example, that my subject at Choate was "underwater exploration"? Read the *Winston-Salem Sentinel* and learn the facts.

After the festivities I flew back to Lost Thyme with Richard's brother and sister, both of whom became enamored of *la vie primitive* here and confessed, before leaving for London, that they preferred Lost Thyme to all the sumptuous North Carolina manor houses they've been exposed to. It was sweet of them to pay me such an extravagant tribute, but I really believe it was the *haute cuisine*, the gorgeous crisp air, the loquacious stream, the infinitude of wild flowers and singing birds which impressed them ponderously.

I stay here until the 5th, when, *deo volente*, I head back to That Place for a six-week summer stint. Who knows, the gods may be propitious and I may, ere the leaves turn, see you in your own lovely bailiwick.

Yours,

J.J.

❦⸺❧

That same June we had John Joseph over for dinner before our annual trip to Norway. A casual question of mine about the origin of the word "collop" was just the sort of thing to get him going on a research project. John Joseph loved to do research, and the odder the better. He had many volumes of reference books and, of course, there was the school library.

LOST THYME
LABOR DAY, 70
{ TO ARMONK }
Très chère madame,

Swifter than whirlwinds the summer hath passed. Albeit I had these notes prepared some time ago, I did not, alas, find time to knit them together into the Monograph I had promised you. But pour over these notes. Now you and I have something terribly arcane that we share: omniscience regarding collops, concerning which, only yesterday, we were both colossally ignorant. I devoutly hope the Notes will amuse you as much as they will instruct you.

How was Norway? Did the time there, too, flee with a kind of mad, tormented rush? Here it is autumn already: the temperature is right now in the upper forties, but delicious, and the last of the orchids, the ladies' tresses, abloom in the swamp, where soon the fringed gentian will appear with all their subtle and mysterious beauty. I had a long weekend with the sybarites of Fishers Island as a house-guest of the R. E. T. Hunters. A dinner-party every night at some house or other: the last stronghold of the American plutocracy.

Up here in my woods I have been absolutely inundated with guests—continuously. One night I returned from the Boston Symphony in Lenox to find, asleep in cars in my driveway, seven unexpected guests! And yesterday I had five. What once was an isolated outpost seems to have become a crossroads.

Today I shall pot a maidenhair fern or two for you. Be sure to pick up the pot when you appear at Choate next week.

Love, etc.

J.J.

And here are his notes, the extraordinary fruit of his research on "collops."

Dedicated to très chère madame, la duchesse de Neset:
Notes for a Monograph on Collops

ALTERNATE SPELLING	*colope, colhoppe, coloppe, colloppe, colep, colyp, colop, colup, collup, collop, collopp, collope, collop.*
ORIGIN	Unknown
COGNATES	The Swedish Kalops: slices of beef, stewed The German Klops: beaten meat, a steak

I. ITS FIRST MEANING: an egg fried on bacon, fried ham and eggs

EARLY OCCURRENCES

1362:	Langland's *Piers Ploughman*, VII, 272:
	"I have no salt Bacon, ne no Cokeneges, bi Crist Colopus to maken."
	Ibid. XVL, 67
	"And ete many sondry metes...bacon and colhoppes"
1530:	Palsgr.: "Collope, meate, *oeuf au Lard*"
1542:	Boorde, *Dyetary*, XVI:
	"Bacon is good for carters and plowmen . . . but and yf they have the stone, coloppes and eggs is as holesome for them as a talowe candell is for a horse mouth."
1599:	Porter, *Angry Wom. Abingd.*, 105:
	"Ile cut thee out in collops and egges, in steakes, in sliste beef, and frye thee with the fyer."
1611:	Cotgr. *Des oeufs á la riblette*:
	" . . . egges and collopps; or an Omelet or Pancake of egges
and	slices of bacon mingled, and fried together."
1681:	W. Robertson:
	"Collops and eggs, for dinner."
1877:	N. W. Linc. Gloss:
	"Collops and eggs, fried bacon and eggs."

II. "COLLOP MONDAY": The day before Shrove Tuesday, on which fried bacon and eggs still form the appropriate dish in many places.

1769:   De Foe: *Tour Gt. Brit.* III, 300:
"The Monday preceding Fastens Even...called everywhere in the North Collop Monday, from an immemorial custom there of dining that day on Collops and Eggs."

1805:   R. Anderson:
"The first Monday before Lent is called Collop Monday; and the first Tuesday Pancake Tuesday."

III. A SLICE OF MEAT FRIED (MIXA) OR BROILED (CARBONELLA)

1440:   Collope, frixitura, in frigo, carbonacium, carbonella.

1583:   Stonyhurst's translation of *Aeneid.* I, 24:
"Soom doe slise out collops on spits yeet quirilye trembling."

1660:   Blount, *Boscobel,* 35:
"His Majesty cut some of into Collops, called for a frying-pan and butter, and fry'd the collops himself."

IV. A SLICE OF MEAT: WITHOUT ANY REFERENCE
TO MODE OF COOKING

1577:   Holinshed *Chronicles,* II, 19
"If a man, saie they, had eaten a collop of Adam his leg, he had eaten flesh."

1641:   ". . . they would not kill any English beast and then eat it, but they eat Collops out of them being alive."

1681:   "Collope of live-horses hips . . . " [*Ugh!*]

1741: "Cut your Plaice in six Collops . . ."

1845: Thackeray: "I have often cut off great collops of the smoking beares."

1855: Whitby Glossary: a threat of chastisement to children:"I'll cut you into collops."

V. A FIGURATIVE USE FROM 1795: G. Wakefield
"Interlarded with nauseous collops of self-applause." [*I like that one!*]

VI. MEAT CUT INTO SMALL PIECES:

1730: "Scotch collopc: a savoury dish made of slic'd veal, bacon, forc'd meat and several other ingredients."

1850: W. Irving: ". . . collops with onion sauce." [*Now steak with onions.*]

1863: London Times, 6 April: "The beefsteaks minced and stewed become 'hot collops'."

VII. A PIECE OF FLESH, FIGURATIVELY:

1562: Heywood: "It is a deere colup that is cut out of th'owne flesh."

1631: J. Donne "that a Martyr . . . shd. send me . . . a collop of his flesh wrapped up in a half-sheet of paper." [*Ugh, again!*]

Shakespeare: "To say this boy were like me . . . most dearest, my collop."

1515:   Bible (Geneva): "He hathe covered his face with his fatnes, and hath collops in his flancke..."

IX. [*A repulsive use of the term*]:
A CLOT OF MUCUS FROM THE NOSE OR THROAT:

1589:   ". . . a collop that dropt out of Mydas nose."
1611:   ". . . a collop of flegme spet out . . ." etc. etc.

In the spring of 1971, Harry and I bought an apartment in the just-finished UN Plaza. Around the same time our eldest son, Rikk, informed us that he was getting married two weeks after he graduated from Williams College, a date that was imminent. Shortly before this had been announced, I had begun to realize that my overpowering need to be the center of attention had infuriated my children and that I had assumed a strident, brittle-edged tone with them. They let me know about it and I knew they were right, still it upset me, and I'd often feel so low I would look myself up in the telephone directory to see if I existed. I had written to John Joseph that I had fallen into a depression and I couldn't find life exhilarating and joyful. John Joseph must have been extremely disappointed in me for this May, 1971 letter is the only one in all his correspondence in which he addresses me as "Patricia" and signs his name "John."

{ TO U.N. PLAZA, NY }
Dear Patricia,

This letter is a reprimand to you; for I saw you yesterday as I have not before seen you and as I want never again to see you: dour, perturbed, anxious. Life is too short for such extravagances and luxuries as despondency and despair. You have, God knows, blessings (and I do *not* mean material blessings) enough to keep you in a state of joyous gratitude. I am aware that my spouting may strike you as gratuitous and platitudinous, but allow me to spout: the source of your grief, if grief it may be called, is a situation morally and legally out of your hands, beyond your jurisdiction; therefore make it emotionally beyond you. I refer, of course, to Rikk. Let him follow whatever patterns he wishes. If they strike you as egregiously odd, then they are odd; and that is the end of it. After all, he is fundamentally a sound, honest, wholesome human being; and his idiosyncrasies are his, as yours are yours and mine mine. The important detail is this: he is your son. Love him. And love him not in spite of the idiosyncrasies, but with them, even because of them. And remember always that you are not the first mother-in-law in history with a daughter-in-law problem. So relax. Think of the other boys, of Harry; of your excitement in the myriad delights the world offers—human contacts, music, poetry, the wondrous beauty of nature and of certain cities, Rome, Stowe, Armonk—even the dilapidated and seedy Gables. Thou hast, my sweet, much to be glad about: be glad with a vast and passionate gladness. No more introspections of a melancholy sort, please. No more analyses, no more apprehensions. Go walk in the garden or prowl a turbulent city street or concoct an omelette or open a bottle of Orvieto; and when Harry returns from Amsterdam, throw your arms around him and tell him that you both have vast riches to delight in, to be proud of, and to be grateful for. And with that series of final propositions I bless you.

Yours, etc.
John

❧ ❧

Shortly after his reprimanding letter, we left for Europe. I have always traveled extensively and John Joseph enjoyed traveling vicariously with me.

SUMMERDAY 71
{ TO ARMONK }
Très chère madame,

You are in London? in Oslo? in Manhatten? in Armonk? How was England? Did you, in proper style, attend the races?

Here I am at Shelburne: a rather Scandinavian mid-summer day—mist, pines, birdcalls, rushing stream, and solitude—ah, at last, blessed solitude. For I have been inundated with visitors. (Two have just left, a hippyesque pair living in a tent about a mile away by a beaver dam.) Not that I minded the invasion. *Tout au contraire*, it has been lovely: my weekend guests, gastronomes and venophiles, had what they called a magnificent weekend. But of a sudden the N.E. landscape has become a thick jungle. The orchids were utterly gorgeous, and the giant primulas, about two feet high, were like Dr. Thornton engravings. Herbs are doing well—have even harvested a cup of marjoram. And—I have a dog; a bright, handsome, but extremely possessive Rhodesian Ridgeback which finding no lions to hunt, brings back tortoises. Her bark would freeze your blood. And I do believe she will devour a prowler one day. I am severe with her, but she seems to enjoy discipline. Her name: "Moira," the Greek word for fate, destiny, lot. She's staring—nay, glaring at me as I write, for I have just commanded her to lie on her couch. But enough of me. What of you? When do you retire to Scandinavia? And what are you thinking?

What of the boys?

My best to Harry—and strive always to be serene.

Yours, etc.
John Joseph

❦ ❧

John Joseph also enjoyed describing his life—and his meals—at Lost Thyme, and did so with enormous enthusiasm and great detail, as though he were describing a voyage to exotic lands.

LOST THYME
THE 1ST OF JULY OF 71
{ TO NESET }
Très chère madame,

Lost Thyme could not be lovelier: herbs and ferns flourishing: guests galore—including a pair of marvelous Texans who, besides bringing a case of Beychevelle '66 spent all their time—man and wife—sawing and splitting wood and bathing naked in my brook. And I have that savage dog, the Rhodesian Ridgeback, whom you've met, somewhat acclimated. She's a marvelous watchdog but hyperaffectionate. I cannot move without her following me.

As regards Food (here we go again!) you should taste some of the concoctions which emerge from my primitive kitchen. But I frankly think the loveliest meal was a picnic lunch for the Texans: cucumber sandwiches, crabmeat paste on Finnish rye—crisp, radishes, scallions, plum tomatoes—and iced champagne. It fairly overwhelmed them. But there have been plenty of peasant dishes, Greek *fasolia*, Egyptian *m'jaddarah*, and Lebanese *dolmadas*. Despite all this gastronomy, I have lost 10 pounds; have had my hair utterly shorn; and am as brown as Selassie. Am rereading Agatha Christie and working on a novella you'll never see. (I always burn 'em when I finish.) Have a good holiday. Look about you. Count your blessings. And study to be grateful.

Con amore,

John Joseph

P.S. And now an absolutely magnificent storm is raging: trees swaying, lightning flashing, thunder roaring so as to frighten the poor little lion-killing canine. I'm sure Lear and Fool are outside screaming imprecations against the elements, but I dare not open the door: the electricity will, like an eel, into this old house glide.

FROM *Mr. Joseph at Lost Thyme:*

TO ME, THE WORD SUCCESS—WHICH IS BANDIED ABOUT TOO MUCH—IMPLIES VERY QUIET THINGS. IT IMPLIES BEING AGREEABLY OCCUPIED ALL THE TIME. DOING WHAT YOU SHOULD DO WHEN YOU SHOULD DO IT, AND DOING IT AS WELL AS YOU CAN. IF IT MEANS MIXING A MARTINI, MIXING THE BEST MARTINI. IF IT MEANS BLACKENING YOUR BOOTS, IT MEANS DOING THE BEST JOB WITH YOUR BLACKENED

BOOTS. IF IT MEANS MAKING A SALAD DRESSING, EVEN
THOUGH YOU DO IT EVERY DAY OF THE WEEK, EACH SALAD
DRESSING SHOULD BE THE BEST SALAD DRESSING YOU MAKE.
IF IT MEANS WELCOMING YOUR GUESTS, YOU SHOULD MAKE
EACH GUEST FEEL THAT HE'S THE MOST IMPORTANT MAN IN
THE HOUSE. NOTHING SENSATIONAL...

---

*On a visit to Choate in the spring of 1972, Harry and I brought a picnic
to one of John Joseph's favorite haunts, an apple orchard. On this occasion Edward Albee, who had come to Choate to give a speech, joined us.
John Joseph abhorred paper napkins and paper cups, and so I had
brought white damask napkins and Baccarat wineglasses with a large
white tablecloth and sterling silver cutlery. We sat under the trees where
John Joseph's exuberance overshadowed even the famous playwright,
who leaned against a trunk, content to banter with him occasionally.
A photograph of Leif at the picnic, which shows him, hair long and
clothes unkempt, blowing the downy seeds from a dandelion, captures
the ephemeral quality of the afternoon.*

CHOATE SCHOOL
SUNDAY, 14 MAY 72
{ TO ARMONK }
Felizia carissima,

This is the word: civilized. The number of persons who qualify
for that epithet is so limited as to make one shiver with chagrin.
The other word is vulgar—or barbaric; and the number of persons
who qualify for that epithet is so vast as to make one shudder with
horror. Yesterday was civilized. The *déjeuner aux herbes* was civilized. Mine hosts were civilized, the menu, the wine—of extremely

PATRICIA LARSEN

LEIF BLOWING DANDELION SEEDS AT OUR PICNIC.

civilized quality. For which, thanks, vast thanks. That hill, the almost-blossoming trees, the sun, the small gathering of warm and joyous persons, the idle chatter and the laughter; of such is the really immortal essence composed. Enjoyment of such brief, ephemeral delights makes, paradoxically, the immortal. I shall never forget. Nor shall I be able adequately to thank.

E. A.'s speech that night was blunt: he told the assemblage that their govt., their president, their attitudes towards the arts and politics were not precisely ideal or idyllic. I enjoyed watching some of the wildly conservative conservatives squirm. They must have loathed E. A. Earlier a camera-crew came and—hold your breath—interviewed me; asked what I thought of the "current crop" at Choate; and I unequivocally proclaimed the "current crop" the best ever—unaffected, unmaterialistic, unobsessed (as their fathers were) with fetishes, with labels, with caste symbols. Most importantly of all, I stressed the marvelous fact—nay, the miracle—of this "crop's" capacity for love and kindness. Some of my earlier "crops" will be chagrined. Good.

Yours con amore,
J.J.

SHELBURNE, MASSACHUSETTS
19 JUNE 72
{ TO NESET }
Très chère Patrizia,

Irish weather here: cold, misty, and intensely green. The woods resemble the Amazon jungle. The brook, embarrassed with such a plethora of showers, roars. My garden thrives. All I have lost thus far is one exuberant plant of basil, which some rabbit or woodchuck of laudable gastronomical inclinations has devoured—and enjoyed, I hope.

I have been trying to get the little house "reorganized": finally removed the stove and now enjoy open fires in the living-room, as I do each night in my own bedroom: fires, not for effect, not for atmosphere, but for warmth, damn it. Am reading Edmund Wilson's *Upstate* and a series of essays by Geo. Steiner, plus the usual murder-mystery items to which I constantly revert, driven by some daemon or other in this house who makes one yearn for a shudder or two by candle-light.

I had an enchanting visitor the other day, a doe which either nibbled or sniffed the grass just outside the window. Moira, watching through the window, made the most extraordinary squeaks and gibberings by way of protesting the doe's presence. But the doe did not seem to mind. Each evening at 8:45 punctually my Whipporwill comes, perches on the porch—crouches, not perches—and croaks the approach of nightfall. Wild strawberries are almost ripe. Daisies stud the meadows. My herb-garden snake has grown since last summer. He now knows me. Are you, in Norway, having this Irish climate? Is Per with you? I have the feeling that if he is on this side of the Atlantic, he will pop by.

Tell me what you can about the presence of Runic inscriptions in your part of Norway. Also, has there been much activity in Norwegian bogs? I refer to discoveries of persons buried for two thousand years or so, sacrificial victims usually, and beautifully preserved. The Danes are always encountering them, but I have read in Glob's *The Bog People* that they are found all over Scandinavia.

Love, etc.

J.J.

On the assumption that a large mound in the tun was either the grave of a Viking or a bog person, Harry one summer made a deep trench in it and ruined the surrounding grass only to find a cache of tin cans. Jennie, our cook for many years at Neset, who had a low opinion of men, but not of Harry, said philosophically, "Sann er livet" (that's life), and brought in someone to clean up the mess.

❦

LOST THYME
30 JULY 72
{ TO NESET }
Très chère Patrizia,

Can anything be more poignantly symbolic of the ephermerality of the human condition than the swift passing of this lovely summer? As I inscribed "30 July 72", I had a stab at the heart: and the room re-echoed with a query: "Whither has it gone?" to which I spoke aloud my own query: "What does it all mean?" And an answer came, shrill and clear: "It all means *niente.*" How silly, how wasteful of human energy to act as if it had meaning, how fatuous to take anything seriously, how idiotic, at last, to take one's self seriously. The elements that matter are the triviata, the ubiquitous triviata: The sun, the earth, the greenness, the wild flowers, the birdsongs, the warbling brook, the silences, the laughter. Moira knows: she dozes in the benignant sun, her belly full, her dreams involving who knows what lions of yore?

Sunday morning: *no* guests—in the house, that is. Yesterday, totally uninvited and unexpected, a girl from Boston arrived with a British chap, but she did not want the hospitality of the house. They'd brought sleeping-bags (*For Whom the Bell Tolls!*) and a basket of fruit for supper. After bathing in the brook they took to the hills, where they still sleep or where the mountain-lions have eaten them.

I had a small dinner last night for three, and the meal came largely from the earth: *Tripa à la Firenze* (pure heaven!), wild purslane with Parmesan cheese, assorted greens from the garden, and a salad, cheese (local) and apples (local). I must teach you to concoct the *tripa*. It will suggest, the moment you catch its aroma, the Ponte Vecchio and the Duomo, if not the mud of the Arno.

But, alas, the summer flees: goldenrod thrives and habenaria orchids begin to bloom along the brookbank in the woods: and no robins feed on the lawn: and the last of three families of swallows has left the nest on the porch: and the evenings are sparkling: and the mornings are cold enough for the fires: and the singing insects (they who carol the end of summer) are heard at night: and the fireflies are gone: and time, swift relentless time flees.

Yours, etc,

John Joseph

❦ ❦

The following summer of 1973 I was alone most of the time, spending much of each day drawing and painting wild flower illustrations for a scrapbook-diary of Neset, which recounted snippets of our and the children's lives during the Norwegian summers. I grew absorbed by all the different wild flowers and asked John Joseph for some of the names.

LOST THYME
28 JULY 73
{ TO NESET }
My dear Patrizia

The little book on wild flowers is down there in the south at a place called Wallingford, to which one of these days I must make a

JOHN JOSEPH AND GUESTS WITH HIS BELOVED DOG, MOIRA.

visit, at which time I shall recover for you the book in which you will find local names for some of the blossoms you've checked.

Your solitude: hold on to it, clutch it, wring from it every last drop of bliss. The solitudinous state: what an enviable condition, and what a rare one; and how few the persons capable of handling it, talented or gifted enough to enjoy it; and the mystery of beginning and ending life in the solitudinous state.

Your friend Richard Hunter was here from Monday to Thursday: spent most of the time reading; a bit of melancholy clinging to him; and he is palpably disturbed at being jobless, though he hopes Mr. Dey of Choate will re-engage him.

I spend a good segment of each day in the vegetable garden, and I have already feasted on tomatoes, cucumbers, lettuces, radishes, spinach, and all the herbs. Made a *ziti al pesto* last night which consumed a huge parcel of basil; and the ziti was followed by a cold boiled chicken covered, absolutely, with a sauce derived from mayonnaise wedded to horse radish derived from the good earth: followed by *les premiers haricot-verts au beurre*: followed by Vermont cheese: followed by fresh raspberries picked in the afternoon. As you have guessed, there is a minimum of solitude hereabouts, but I complain not, since I know there are no guest-rooms in the tomb.

A bright radiant day: A bientôt.

Yours, etc.
J.J.

Richard had been divorced by his wife after a marriage of only three years. Upon his marriage he had left his teaching post at Choate, and, though wanting later to teach again, had not been re-engaged there.

❀-❀

To alleviate Harry's constant travel to Europe we had rented a flat in London on Upper Grosvenor Street. The decorator of our flat used the word "squab," a word I found mysterious, and I asked John Joseph what it meant.

CHOATE SCHOOL
5 DECEMBER 73
{ TO ARMONK }
My dear Patrizia,

As early as 1664 "squab" was a word for a couch or an ottoman. In 1710 Pope wrote: deliciously:

"On her large squab you find her spread

Like a fat corpse upon a bed."

As early as 1687 "squab" meant, too, a thick or soft cushion, serving to cover the seat of a chair or of a sofa. And, as you have discovered, decorators still use the word; British decorators, I mean, with a penchant for lovely infrequently encountered archaisms. I do not see a Manhattan decorator using the word, do you?

Please believe me to be, Madam, always sincerely,

Yours, etc.
John Joseph

LOST THYME
1 JAN 74: MORNING
{ TO ARMONK }
To Patrizia, salutations:

"Snug" is a word which has had for me, comfortable, cute, homey, vulgar, repulsive connotations. But (God forgive me) here I am about to use it to describe the life here at the microscopic house, now that heat and lights have, amid the "energy crisis," finally appeared. Yes; "snug" is the word; and what suggests that awful epithet is a glimpse, through the windows, of the world outside: snow, ice, sleet, leaden skies, half-frozen brook, a grim and wintry world, whereas here there are warmth and lights, and freshly peeled oranges for breakfast with a pot of Indian tea awaiting me steaming and hot (and there is Mozart on the FM). In any case, here I am; and it is lovely.

What I find most appealing is the utter solitude and, occasionally, I am struck with the fantastic allure of silence. Every now and then a neighbor pops in, all of them delighted to see the small house alive, as in summer, but my neighbors are all young and beautiful and helpful. You should see them sweeping and vacuuming and dusting and even gathering the laundry to do it for me. And one of them wants to make new curtains (*without* pelmets!). I putter, I walk, I read; and what a plan for reading, or should I say rereading, for I am doing, for the nth time, *Anna Karenina* and *Tess* (I must have a thing for "fallen women"), but I am also deep in a biography of Thomas More, who must have been one of the really extraordinarily *good* persons of all times. And as for the world "out there," I really can't say that I can believe it exists. Lord, what a stuffy eremite I'm going to be!

Con amore,
J.

17 APRIL 74
{ TO 46 UPPER GROSVENOR ST., LONDON }
My dear Patrizia,

This is a letter I shall regret writing but a letter I cannot resist writing: and I beg you to forgive me if the letter brings you a bit of uneasiness or even grief. But the fact is I suddenly find myself in hospital, awaiting surgery. Even as I write the words, I grow numb and incredulous; but here I be and here I wait. Oddly enough, my "condition" was discovered primarily because of my vanity. I was asking the School doctor, who was giving me a routine checkup, to scold me for having put on weight. But he nodded grimly and said he thought it was not fat; and so there were x-rays and a visit to a specialist and here I am: a faulty bladder and kidneys, but—here's the irony—absolutely without distress or pain. I say to myself as I write these lines, "Tear the paper up, John," but somehow I don't. And though I wish not to disturb you, I remind myself that silence is not what you'd like.

The horrors were at night. The dourest, the bleakest prospects appear. And always the indisputable truth: one is at last facing death squarely. There are no more games. And one realizes how base it is to feel sorry for oneself, and goes on feeling sorry. Or angry. Or inwardly chuckling at the irony. And those visitors who come to console bring up the future, "when it will all be behind you," little realizing that one's sense of time is injured in such a way as to make impossible a projection into the future. And, oddly enough, there is no past: there's only this heavy, frightening, almost unbearable Now. I have never been known for my heroics, and so this despair seems somehow natural.

I know that my outpouring of woe should embarrass me as much as it may chagrin you; but, to prove there's a spark of humor left within me, don't you find it bizarre that the only pen I can find writes in red ink and the only paper is yellow?

Con amore,
John Joseph

In his video *Mr. Joseph at Lost Thyme*, Monty Hunter asked John Joseph why he was so direct with his feelings:

I AM DIRECT BECAUSE I HAVE RESPECT FOR THE TRUTH. I'VE ALWAYS, WITH MY MOTHER, BELIEVED THAT ONE SHOULD SAY PRECISELY WHAT ONE MEANS, AND SAY IT AS BRIEFLY AND AS TERSELY AS POSSIBLE, SO THAT THERE'S NO POSSIBILITY OF A MISUNDERSTANDING. AVOID CIRCUMLOCUTIONS, AVOID EUPHEMISMS, AVOID TAUTOLOGIES, JUST BE DIRECT; EVEN AT THE RISK OF SHOCKING. FOR EXAMPLE, THE WORD "DEATH" WE ALWAYS USED. WE NEVER USED "PASSED AWAY" OR "PASSED ON" OR "CROSSED OVER."

SHELBURNE, MA.
18 JUNE 74
(TO NESET)
Patrizia carissima

When I reached Shelburne Sunday night, I tried telephoning you. But, because of electric storms, no telephone service. Today, upon restoration of service, I telephoned, and learned that you'd left at 7:00 a.m. this day for Norway—and that (astonished I was to learn) you propose to return in July.

I am *not* at Lost Thyme. I am with friends who live a couple of miles away. They literally abducted me on Sunday evening, and here I am in the loveliest of bucolic settings (chickens outside, a horse galloping about) trying to recover. And I think I'm already better!

Weather here superb: cool and bright, the family charming and all love. I have the most incredible room whose four walls of pink brick and timbers were discovered, only recently, under 19th century plaster. When I awaken in the morning, I fully expect to be greeted by Geoffrey Chaucer or Piers the Ploughman.

Strawberries are ripe: the children have gone off to a farm to harvest them. Mrs. T. is an excellent cook and every meal is something a bit better than ordinary. I help now and then.

Have a peaceful holiday there in Norway.

Con amore, yours,

John Joseph

LOST THYME
7 AUGUST 74
{ TO NESET }
Patrizia carissima,

What infinite riches: three communications from you on the same day. I lunched on the terrace, I got fitted for a fall suit on Saville Row, I killed a salmon, I supped and wined in Irish castles, and I even turned my knee-cap. What empathy. You are having a summer rich and diverse, despite your tiny querulous note of "creeping depression." Listen, me love: if you have your health, you've got it all; depressions are a loathsome luxury. I forget which of the English nobs had this as his motto, but never believe it to be meaningless: *sine sanitate nullas felicitas.* At the risk of offending the unknown English nob, that has become my motto: without health, no felicity.

And here I am in the little house in the jungle. I can see, each day, the vines creeping closer and closer; in no time they will have strangled the little house. Oddly enough, the veg. garden which my sweet neighbors put in for me is flourishing, and I am giving away squashes, lettuces, beets, etc. Also, I am becoming an avid vegetarian.

I was down in Meriden yesterday for a session with my surgeon, who had good and cheering things to tell me after examining me. I improve, though I have a way to travel before resuming my climbs and my 6-7 miles of walking.

This was the summer I was to have spent on the Swedish Island of Gotland. What an irony. How correct I have been never to formulate plans.

Con amore,
Yours, etc.
John Joseph

❦

In December of 1974, Harry and I gave John Joseph a round-trip ticket to London for a Christmas present.

OXFORD
CHRISTMAS EVE, 74
{ TO STOWE, VERMONT }
My dear Patrizia,

You will not believe a syllable inscribed on this page. Here goes: I have just picked garden roses, aenemones, blooming rosemary (I've never seen it *abloom* before) and other flowers for the table. I have worn sun-glasses all day. I have *not* put on my topcoat. Oxford is as lovely today as the 18th century admirers of the town proclaimed it to be in June. Exotica of all sorts bloom in the gardens of this part of town and I wish violently to swipe 'em. (I don't even know their names.) The aerial crossing was swift, we arrived at Heathrow 3o minutes early. There was *not one soul* at Heathrow: except my friend from Oxford, waiting to drive me northwards. Got here and we all had champagne and fresh caviar before going to bed. For them it was after midnight; for me not yet suppertime. *Merci infiniement.*

Con amore,
John Joseph

LOST THYME
MONDAY
23 JUNE 75
{ TO ARMONK }
Patrizia carissima,

I suspect that you are still around, for the weather persists in being (and it's the only, albeit vulgar, word for it) gorgeous. The other night when I took my walk, I felt far superior to that male who, on alighting on the moon, said, "One small step for man!" For no moonscape could possibly compare with these green hills and blue skies, slightly pinked by the sunset, the air so intensely clear that one could literally make out clumps of pine needles in profile against the sky on the hilltops. Then there was that ineffable loneliness: only the faraway barking of a farm dog, like a prop out of Turgenev, to remind one that human creatures did inhabit the place. Indeed, it is no accident that I constantly read Turgenev up here. I devoutly hope, one day, to meet him (or his benign poltergeist) emerging from the woods, with a gamebag filled with grouse. And the aromas: it is the height of the *rosa floribunda* season here; they grow wild everywhere, like heather in Britain, and throw off a delicate most cool and delicious smell.

I finished my walk at the farmhouse of friends who are always surrounded by their children and children's friends, college-age; where I am the perennial Uncle John, for whom champagne is immediately opened: the friends who undertook to "kidnap" me from the Gables last year. and put themselves to work healing me: lovely, enchanting persons.

It is early morning, the sun is glorious. Chicken livers and mushrooms are on the stove. A pot of tea lies waiting.

Believe me, madam, to be ever devotedly and sincerely

Yours, etc.

John Joseph

LOST THYME

27 JULY 75

{ TO NESET }

Patrizia carissima,

The cold chablis days are back: and this is to express the hope that you are having them in Norway, where, by this time, I suspect you are. My English friends have done nothing but extol the enchantment of the climate in England this summer.

I had guests from Lenox yesterday and one of them insisted on doing the lawn-cutting here with the result that this morning's air, cool and Octoberish, is most heavily scented with the incomparable aroma of sweet grass, mint, balm, etc. It's like a gigantic herb-spray.

Albeit I have company now and then, I have been solitary much of the time—in training, so to speak, for "retirement"; and the one feature of living a solitary life that is amusing and ironic is this: I tend to develop what one of my M.D.'s calls "tranquillity asthenia"—a feeling of fatigue or weakness springs from having "nothing" to do and "no one" to speak with. I am, naturally, vitally concerned with this fancily named defect, "tranquillity asthenia," for it can make the difference between settling here in this divine valley and leasing a furnished room on Eighth Avenue. We shall see.

The veg. garden feeds both me and some of the beasties which reminds me: pay no attention to those "ecologists"; wild life was never more flourishing. The most divine white orchid is in blossom right now beside my parked car. My best to Harry. And believe me to be ever devotedly and sincerely

Yours, etc.
John Joseph

LOST THYME
10 AUGUST 75
{ TO NESET }
Patrizia suae carissimae salutem dat:

Summer evening at Shelburne, the brook raging (we've had two days of pelting rains, now gone), birdcalls not so clamorous as they were, blackberries ripe and plum-sized, the garden teeming with edibles (and weeds). Last night it was cold enough for a steep blaze in the fireplace; not so this night. And as for summer, I've idled it away: which is what summers were meant for—pure idling, idling *sans* remorse, *sans* regret, *sans* guilt.

Of company I have had much: but company, I find, something of a therapeutic, getting oneself out of oneself. Your letters, too, have been a therapeutic, enabling me, albeit vicariously, to visit London theatre, Stourhead, and now the cool tranquillity of Norway. Why you ever return to New York I cannot see, but then I was ever myopic.

I have had a visit with the doctor, who urges me *not* to retire this year, who predicts that, at this stage, I should find it excessively traumatic. In short, he urges me not to quit until I am closer than I am to being "fit," whatever that is. I haven't really been "fit" because of the abhorrent tablets I have to take: a side-effect, he tells me, is this weakness. No pain, thank God, but an almost delicious asthenia, a somewhat Chekhovian lassitude. Appetite good: plenty of wines: and as congenial as can be: and one's visitors keep telling one how marvelous one looks. So I look fit; and that, I daresay, is something to crow over.

A guest is cutting the grass and the house is being slowly drenched with the odour of sweetgrass. It is such summer smells that enrich the summer for me. Centuries ago I must have had a life on this planet, a wholly rural life, an absolutely unurban one: for there's a powerful *nostalgic* accompanying the infiltration of the odour.

I've been cooking many things from the garden, particularly stuffed squashes, and vineleaves (*dolmadas*), and *al pesto*, and gorgeous *haricots verts* (but they are *jaunes*) and *betteraves* and salads of every type, covered with marjoram, thyme, basil, mint, parsley, and tarragon.

This will find you, *j'espère*, enjoying hugely your summer in the cool Norwegian farmland and writing your book and painting your little pictures and dreaming your dreams. And so I close, reminding you, *très chère* Patrizia, that I am always loyally and devotedly and gratefully

Yours, etc.
John Joseph

❦—❦

I had consulted a psychiatrist about my "creeping depression," but our sessions were not productive and I soon gave them up. John Joseph was pleased as he had no use for "psyche-men."

My dear Patrizia,

It delights me enormously that your patience with the psyche-man was ephemeral. Your scorn, your contempt, your distrust I share. I resent the implication that, for all their training, they can explore the most elusive and mysterious and divine element within us—the psyche. And I mean "divine" literally: it requireth a God to create anything as complicated and as unfathomable as the psyche. Therefore, I even see something blasphemous in their presuming to comprehend the psyche. (What, anyway, is a "normal" psyche? And who decides on the attributive "normal"?) Fuck the psyche-man, I say: live, be joyous, work, be troubled when troubles arise, but be aware that in God's great scheme of things *nothing* matters: and if you think I spout, remember that Death, sweet Death, lies lurking in the lilac bushes to prove that nothing matters: neither accomplishment, nor riches, nor fame—but most of all egocentricity; for one must be inordinately self-aware to think that his or her ego must be put under a glass, studied, stretched, perforated, "analysed." And when the psyche-men start handing out their magical pills, they declare most affirmatively their real significance: witches and wizards.

Now go off and prune more trees; exhaust yourself; nap; read something; have a drink; and command the Admirable Wong to concoct something light and delicate to accompany that chilled Chablis. And never forget, Madam, that I am ever yours devotedly and gratefully etc.

John Joseph

The "Admirable Wong" was our Chinese cook. Whenever John Joseph was coming for a meal, Wong would start chopping at 6 a.m. instead of 7 a.m. Occasionally, when I suggested a dish, Wong would say scornfully, "that ship-side food," which meant it wasn't good enough for John Joseph, who was mutually an ardent admirer of Wong.

❧⚬❧

In early 1975 we moved from our flat on Upper Grosvenor Street to a narrow six-story townhouse on Chesterfield Hill, which belonged to International Utilities, an association with which Harry worked. When November came around I had written that I was feeling very sorry for myself as none of the children would join us in England for Thanksgiving and was wondering whether Harry and I should go to the States for the holiday for the sake of "family reunion."

CHOATE SCHOOL
SUNDAY, 2 NOVEMBER 75
{ TO 12 CHESTERFIELD HILL }
Patrizia carissima,

I should like to imagine this epistle will greet you when you enter the front hall of your London house; for I want to reiterate: do not your holiday blast for the sake of seeing children at Thanksgiving time. Nothing would be more maudlin than to indulge in a bit of "homecoming" for the sake of "family reunion." Even the language one uses to depict the event is slightly nausea-making. So have steep joy at Beaulieu and in the Scottish hills and in the London shops, restaurants, and galleries.

I am almost finished with Gerald Brenan's long auto-biographical work *Personal Record*, and the one lesson I long ago learned but which the work reaffirms is this: *vita brevis*. All these marvelous and creative and insane and even insufferable Bloomsberries—where are they all? Totally dead. And only yesterday they were scribbling their books, painting their pictures, and darting from bed to bed. I think only he and old Dorothy Brett out in Taos are left, and what a turbulent, exhilarating crowd they were—bright, stimulating, humorous, revolutionary in their thinking and in their behavior. And now all totally silent, gone, and alas, except by a few folk like me, forgotten. Ergo, *carpe diem*; and don't, in some gushing outburst of altruism mixed with maternalism, rush back to be with the sweet kiddies, who, if they really wished to see you, have had all these months to sacrifice a weekend or a day for a visit—or should I say a few hours?

All my best to Harry: and believe me, Patrizia, ever to be loyally and gratefully

Yours, etc.
John Joseph

We did not go.

❀-❀

While we were in London, our son Peik had two paintings accepted in a group show in Boston.

CHOATE SCHOOL
27 FEB 76

Patrizia carissima,

Methinks you should attend the Boston show. Although boys don't *say* much about such matters, they *think* much; and your presence there, to Peik particularly, would have enormous significance. And to you, too: for you must admit there'll be a sort of glow to your attending your own son's exhibition. God knows you love to go to art shows. Well, here's one "in the family." So go. Amen!

As for spring recess plans, I've made none. Too frequently, alas, the Fates interfere with me: and so I've decided not to make "lead plays" which may invite their interference. And so I go from hour to hour trying to extract from each hour what may or may not be extractable.

I'm still adrift in a sea of biographies. Just finished Sylvia Plath's *Letters.* What *euphoria* she displays throughout; yet a subtle current is there, ominously hinting at the tragic finale. But the bliss she describes in some of her letters is almost beyond enduring: you know it has to snap. I'm now in Hyde's *Oscar Wilde* and discovering a few things about the early Wilde and his family. If you can, acquire for yourself *The Oxford Book of Literary Anecdotes.* What a gem and what a joy. You'll never travel without it. Or sleep in a bed that does not have it on the bedside table. Or do you already know it? Another of my *déjà vues.* It seems that I've commended that book to you earlier.

Ed. Albee has an opening in New Haven next week. He telephoned yesterday and invited me to lunch with him on Sunday. The opening is *Who's Afraid* etc., *but* with Colleen Dewhurst, whom I much esteem. I saw her in N.H. last fall in an odd thing called *Artichoke.* Nothing culinary about it.

My best to Harry. And believe me, madam, to be always

Yours, etc.

John Joseph

❦–❦

In late spring I wrote J. J. and told him I was sad that none of the children would be joining us in Neset that summer.

LOST THYME

21 JUNE 76

{ TO 12 CHESTERFIELD HILL }

My dear Patrizia,

When the radio-announcer mentioned that we had already arrived at the longest day of the year, I felt a sudden sad fall of the heart: whither hath the spring fled? And can it really be that Autumn is the next season? I realize suddenly that my preoccupation with what I call "the language of time" is not such a silly endeavor after all and I realize, further, that I am absolutely right in believing that there is, there can be, *no* time except the present. And so the most significant thing in the world for me at this moment is my scribbling these lines to you; for this moment is the sole block of time that can, at the present, exist. Hobbes, in *Leviathan* states it most succinctly: how right he was.

And while you are reading this, all the delightful street sounds of London are reaching your ears; and after you have read this, you will put on your bonnet, take your walking-stick or your "brolly," and have for yourself an enchanting walk straight out of *Mrs. Dalloway:* Regent Street, Piccadilly, the Green Park, a short stop at Fortnum's, then over to Jermyn Street for soap, and a glance at the junk which is for sale in the shops of the Burlington Arcade; then tea at Brown's, after which a casual inspection of the pictures on sale at the shops on Dover Street; then back to Chesterfield Hill to dress for dinner, which, wherever you have it, will include, *j'espère,* a bit of smoked salmon and a glass of properly chilled Montrachet. And while all that is going on, here I am, the supreme charlatan, trying to live the life Thoreauesque in the primitive old farmhouse that now has hot and cold running water, a copper bath, a toilet, and a telephone. Me for the Hebrides, where these implements of the Devil don't exist! (Or do they?)

But what I wrote to say originally is this: regarding your feeling "sad" in Norway, never forget that being "sad" is an essential condition of each sensitive and sensible person; and "sadness" is usually co-existensive with beauty. Can you imagine the Parthenon *sans* sadness, or Mozart's No. 40? or a Picasso clown? or a Shakespearean sonnet? or whatever? I read every Christmas *Anna Karenina*—for its intrinsic sadness, I believe—which is why I love Chekhov and Turgenev, and I even love this ancient little farmhouse in its lonely forest-enclosed valley because there is something inexpressibly "sad" within its loveliness and lowliness. Even the morning bird-cries have a quality of sadness—not to speak of the lugubrious cooing of the morning doves. So don't mind sadness in Norway. And if the kids aren't there, they aren't supposed to be there, now that each has found his *métier* and wants to be performing it. But *you* are there and the *beauty* is there: Let not, therefore, the "sad" element blind you to the joy and the delight that persist.

Believe me, chère Patrizia, to be always devotedly and sincerely

Yours, etc.

J.J.

My dear Patrizia,

And now, as the sun vanishes and the shadows become precursors of *la nuit* and the coolth of the evening rises from the brook and the smell of the mint-beds fill the air, I decide to write you a line or two from this tranquil and deserted Valley. Although there has been enormous Bermuda heat during the day, the evenings are enchanting; and in the solitude one finds here one approaches that condition sometimes described as "perfect bliss." Silence is such a rich rare thing in this mad and noisy world.

I am rereading Nancy Mitford's old novels, of the '50's, and feel somewhat superannuated, since many of her allusions would be a perfect conundrum to anyone under sixty. (She was 68 when she died: just fancy!) But what a wonderfully fun-loving world she knew: and concurrently with *Don't Tell Alfred* I've been reading the Memoirs of Lady Duff Cooper, who actually slept (and was by Cecil Beaton photographed lying in) Pauline Borghese's bed at the British Embassy on the Rue St. Honoré. I daresay there must be something pathological in this delight I experience in *le passé retrouvé*, but the present world seems somehow vulgar and tawdry in comparison. If I could have an assembly of spirits here this night, I should like to have Nancy Mitford sparring with Evelyn Waugh, and Virginia Woolf with Lytton Strachey. I think I should prefer that quartet to a visitation from Thos. More, Anne Boleyn, and Christopher Marlowe. I need not add that Virginia's *Letters* is on my bedside table and that I revert to it as an old, old, much loved and much longed for friend.

Your letter describing your visit to Rikk's film-making has finally arrived and your description of Richard Hunter as a martini-lusting corpse is hilarious. (Did they feed him those martinis?)

In the house I have acquired a pet, a chipmunk that boldly walks across the rug and does not intimidate my dog, who, I must say, is eminently merciful, for she could, with one clout, drive the chipmunk into wherever chipmunks go when they croak.

I garden; which means I weed. Though the vegetables are retarded, weeds flourish. As for cutting flowers, nature is bountiful; and the day lilies are ostentatious in their red-and-orange garb—almost as ostentatious as my copper and pine bathroom where I, like a decadent Roman emperor, lie in opulent warm soap-suds at the end of the day. I dine abstemiously, but wine well. Chicken-livers this night done in sherry, and consumed with chilled Chablis. On days that I "do" too much I grow fatigued: on days that I "do" too little I am as fresh as a newly emerged Ithacan fig. Did you ever eat a fig from Ithaca?

Yours, etc.

J.

My eldest son, Rikk, was producing a movie called Billy in the Badlands, *which was eventually released theatrically and was also shown on PBS. It won a regional Emmy for Best Entertainment Special. Professional actors played the main roles, but some friends took bit parts. Richard Hunter's was a corpse lying in a coffin, and to keep him still Rikk promised him dry martinis.*

❦⟶❧

For Christmas 1975 we again gave John Joseph the gift of a round-trip ticket to London. We both loved the architecture of Nicholas Hawksmoor (1661-1736), so when John Joseph came in August, he and I went "Hawksmooring." On the day John Joseph describes in this letter, we took the Thames boat down to Greenwich and then had lunch at the Trafalgar Tavern by the river. At the next table were three immaculately dressed gentlemen, one of whom, to our delight, at the end of the meal, took out a gold toothpick. I was so entranced that, on leaving, I knocked a glass of ale onto his Lobb-shod foot. (The following summer I found a gold toothpick at Asprey's on Bond Street and sent it to John Joseph.)

OXFORD

12 AUGUST 76

{ TO NESET }

My dear Patrizia,

What I shall long remember is the tower of St. Anne's in Limehouse, still noble and self-assertive, among the dilapidated, sad, depressed warehouse and lofts. And another remembrance: the three eighteenth-century gentlemen, florid and gourmandising while chatting about Visconti, longevity, and T.V. programs: and you, like Maria Magdalene, washing the feet of one of them with beer: and the enchanting bijou of a house on Chesterfield Hill, which I should *never* leave were it mine: but, most significantly of all, I shall not soon forget that you apparently delayed your departure for Norway a day in order to go Hawksmooring with me. For that my endless gratitude. Seeing you there in London, I realise sharply that you are a London person: it is, in somewhat the same way Armonk is, the logical background, as your activity—in this case, the logical urban background, as

Armonk is the logical rustic one. And so, again, thanks copiously. It was the highlight of my holiday. I shall long hear the swishing of Thames' waters and shall long remember the view of St. Anne's of Limehouse against the London sky.

Always gratefully etc. Yours,
John Joseph

❦·❧

Harry and I had rented a villa in Asolo, Italy, for three weeks, and it was there that we met Freya Stark. I sent the following notes about our stay to John Joseph:

"Through your friend Jane we met Freya Stark over a cup of tea in her apartment. A few days later she called to ask how we were getting along, and I asked her for dinner. It was pouring rain that night, and so Leif volunteered to fetch her. She arrived wearing a vast cloak with a hood. Divested of this she wore a dress that had us all fascinated. It was like no other garment I'd ever seen and seemed to be made of different and contrasting pieces of materials. She told us with pride that she had bought it at an Arab bazaar for only a pound.

Leif accompanied her home, and it was touching to see the old lady in her hooded cloak taking the arm of the young man who was sheltering her with an umbrella. As they moved off down the steep path, just wide enough for one, I could hear them talk about the crocuses that grew along the edge."

CHOATE SCHOOL
15 SEPTEMBER 76
{ TO 12 CHESTERFIELD HILL }
Patrizia carissima,

Freya Stark: I think she has not written a word I have not read. What a life she has had: one of those 18th century Englishwomen, the kind that used to run off and marry Arab princes and live in deserts; but there was always a kind of primness about her that limited her adventures to the mind and to the eye. I have photographs of her (in one of her books) as a wee tot and she was quite lovely then. And long ago I read of her Asolo life. And there you are tea-ing with her. You *do* find yourself in odd but enviable situations.

Today classes were resumed; and half the morning passed, and I survive. In England I learned to walk great distances again, and am still trying to walk as much as possible. How I missed it the past two years. And what a grave disappointment not walking with you in London, walking in the manner of V. Woolf, savoring every whiff of the London atmosphere. But the barge was memorable, and I can still see St. Anne's of Limehouse gleaming above the squalor and the decrepitude of Limehouse.

My fondest regards to Harry et al. if they are still with you.

Yours, etc.

John Joseph

CHOATE SCHOOL
22 SEPTEMBER 76
{ TO 12 CHESTERFIELD HILL }
Patrizia carissima,

How singularly odd: right after writing you, I encountered Desmond Guinness's *Palladio* and there, in full glory, were the Villa Maser, the Veronese frescoes, and the Teatro Olimpico (what a weird atmosphere the last pours forth). I do have a superb thing on "Capability" Brown which covers *all* of his myriad accomplishments: and learned that he was called "Capability" not because *he* was capable but because he was constantly referring to the "capability" of the landscape upon which he practiced his craft. My, my, my how architectural I've become. These books on my bedside table: the Hawksmoor, the Palladio, and the Brown. Guess I'll go off and build meself a log cabin a la Palladio. (His *real* name was dalla Gondola—prophetic of his activities in Venice, no? like Unity Mitford's name Valkyrie—prophetic of her passion for that mad Wagnerian, Hitler.)

Back to me labours: and have lost me English vigour. I daresay I simply am too much devoted to "loafing" to apply meself to daily labours. How excessively tedious. Am rereading *Emma* these nights. *That* was my era: the 18th century, the era of those three chubby diners at the Trafalgar Tavern. And stay in London as long as you can. Life on this side of the water is dull. Me best to Harry.

Con amore,
Giovanni

CHOATE SCHOOL
20 NOVEMBER 76
{ TO 12 CHESTERFIELD HILL }
Patrizia carissima,

I've been soaking up biographical things: your book on Violet Trefusis casts a rather agreeable light on her, for neither Nigel Nicolson's book nor Acton's book is eminently kind to her. (Acton writes about her in his memoir on Nancy Mitford!) And two days ago I found and read Nancy Peter's book on her father Roger Ackerly. D'you know the Roger Ackerly saga—how he managed two domiciles and two families quite close to each other just outside London and was dearly loved by both ménages? The first study on Roger is by his son, Joe Ackerly, a very important name in literary London, for he published, for years, *The Listener*. His study is quite a shocker and many of his friends have, since Joe's death, wished Joe had not allowed it to be published—*post mortem.*

Exams and reports are upon us: which means I'm having a delightful "loaf," I've been cooking devoutly for troops of my "last class" and some of the meals have been rather *exquises.* I may go up to Shelburne for the holiday: then again I may not: it is good holing up here with everyone away. ("O the peace when the loved ones have departed!")

Always, madam, your
JJ

❦⟶

In January 1977 I suffered a stroke. My balance was affected, and I started to totter. My right arm would bend at the elbow and crook away from my body. If I didn't consciously hold it down by my side, it started to bend and rise up slowly. Also, my writing had become almost illegible. I could not follow the ruled lines of a paper, and, after writing a few sentences, my hand and arm would ache. Worst of all, I found it a great strain to talk. After a few minutes of conversation, I was exhausted. I learned not to try to tell an involved story or express a complicated thought. Although what I wanted to say was clear in my mind, I could not put it into words without the frustration of losing the train of ideas or words to couch them in. Instead of "Good morning," I'd say "Thank you."

Pre-stroke, I could express myself freely, but my inability to do so now struck at the core of my personality. (My daughter, Siri, remarked that I was nicer after the stroke. Perhaps because with my speech difficulties, it wasn't so easy to make cutting remarks!) It was five months after the stroke when I made my first amusing remark. I was with a group of volunteers who were discussing ways to raise money for the

New York City Ballet. The director, Lincoln Kirsten, was a brilliant and forbidding figure. The group decided to have a sweepstakes, and the first prize should be lunch with the director. I said, "Why don't you have the first prize be not to have lunch with him?" Everyone laughed. I was astonished and exultant.

It was only a year after the stroke that I suddenly realized that I was sometimes talking without having to think ahead. It was intoxicating. I also was able to write again.

CHOATE SCHOOL
5 MAY 77
{ TO 12 CHESTERFIELD HILL }
Patrizia Carissima,

How the benign deities favored us last Saturday; what utterly celestial weather, what an efflorescence, what tranquillity. And how good seeing you looking even much better than what is referred to as your "old self." Go on doing those exercises, and you'll wind up a chorus girl. You never looked lovelier. Ditto, Harry.

Tuesday evening I found myself in Manhattan, at a party given to Choate's triad of retirées. There were literally hundreds there and I was never so copiously embraced and kissed and thanked (for what?): it was tantamount to attending me own wake. All that was lacking was some good dour Irish keening. They gave me a pewter dish to mark the occasion with. Manhattan seemed a madhouse, an exceedingly cacophonous madhouse; and I realized that the silences and solitude of Shelburne are a sampling of moments on Parnassus or in the Vale of Tempe. I still have packing and moving and giving away and destroying to look forward to before leaving these no longer warm and soothing shores. I shall be, *deo volente,* intoxicated with sheer bliss when I depart. Go and look at St. Anne's in Soho for me.

And all me love, me undying love,

Yours, etc.
John Joseph

After 33 years of teaching, John Joseph retired from Choate.

❧ ❧

I had sent John Joseph a gold toothpick I had found, which like Proust's madeleine, aroused memories of our wonderful day "Hawksmooring" the year before.

CHOATE SCHOOL
5 JUNE 77
{ TO ARMONK }
Patrizia Carissima,

Such a tiny object: but what magical power it hath; for I have only to touch it and lo, there's St. Anne's of Limehouse and all those lovely masterpieces at Greenwich, and two novices in architecture adaze and incredulous and exhilarated: then the Adam dining room of the Trafalgar Tavern: and whitebait and salmon: and Patrizia spilling ale on the impeccable flannels of the ruddy County Squire, who, *deo gratias,* is enjoying a copious lunch sans worrying about calories and carbohydrates: and champagne for him and his fellow Squires throughout lunch. Then the moment: the appearance of the solid-gold toothpick. And we two provincials watch with rapture and delight. And now I hold mine in my hands, and the magic starts. (Who says there is *no* magic? Poor blind fools!)

I have no elegant Adam dining-salon in which to display ostentatiously this loveliest of things: but I am using it; and every time I touch it, lo, the magic: the 18th century again, the age of elegance; all modern woes and miseries forgotten; even the horrors of packing and cleaning up vanished; and I half expect to hear Nick Hawksmoor prowling in the hallway outside the door.

So you see, my dear Patrizia, not a gift, not a utensil, not a gadget, but a talisman, gushing forth magic lavishly; and I experience wonders and delights rare and unwonted. Ergo, slim, slim indeed are those words "thank you!"

Con amore,
John Joseph

This was the last letter written from Choate School; all subsequent letters were written from Lost Thyme. In the years to follow, as John Joseph settled into his retirement, his letters became longer and even more eloquent.

❧ ⇠ ❧

Harry and I would celebrate our 35th wedding anniversary on 9 July 1977.

7.7.77
{ TO NESET }
My dear Patrizia and Harry,

Although "thirty-five" seems a relatively high number, thirty-five years can pass with the twinkle of an eye, particularly when they have been rich and full and varied. I recall that when my parents celebrated their sixty-fifth anniversary, I asked my father with some irony, how he was able to pass such a span of time with one woman. I shall never forget the look he gave me, nor shall I forget the sweetness of his voice when he gave this answer: "I met her only yesterday." I'm certain that you are both better equipped to comprehend his meaning than I: for each of you met the other only this morning. Please observe that I am religiously avoiding the word "congratulation," a silly word that normally covers a multitude of sins. Please observe, further, that I summon your attention to some of your attainments of thirty-five years: those splendid, if at times erratic (in the Latin sense), children; all their creativity; their total lack of affectation; their icy and rigorous honesty; their warmth and kindness. (I cannot forget that after my surgery, when I thought I was lying on me death-bed, Per *flew* down to Meriden to cheer me up. Although my room was closed to visitors, when the nurse told me who'd come to see me, I practically recovered on the spot.)

Nor can I forget that some of the really charming moments of my life have passed with you two: those elegant picnics under the appleblossoms; those exquisite lunches on the porch; even a crossing of the Atlantic with Harry a few years back; and that unforgettable barge-ride down to Trafalgar Tavern at Greenwich, which will forever connote, for me, golden toothpicks.

When I delivered my Commencement Address in June, my theme was borrowed from *Leviathan:* viz., that there *is* no past (except memories) and there *is* no future, there is only the present. Ergo, reach out and clutch at the present, a marvelous, miraculous, tumultuous, divine gift. Reach out for the present and thank the benign deities who, up there on Olympus, arranged that you two should be affinities. And please believe that you always have the devotion and the affection of this aged hermit of the Shelburne backwoods.

John Joseph

FROM *Mr. Joseph at Lost Thyme:*

THIS BUSINESS OF IGNORING THE PRESENT, RELYING ON THE FUTURE—LINGUISTICALLY, THE FUTURE CANNOT EXIST RIGHT NOW. IT'S STUPID TO SAY THE FUTURE IS, THE FUTURE MAY BE. AND THE SUBJUNCTIVE MOOD LIES IN THE FUTURE; IT MAY NOT BE. SOMETIMES THE FUTURE WILL BE, SOMETIMES EVEN SHALL BE, BUT THE FUTURE DOES NOT EXIST. AND THE PAST DOES NOT EXIST. SO THERE ARE TWO SINS THAT MODERN MAN IS AFFLICTED WITH, ONE IS HE DOTES ON THE PAST. HE DEVOTES TOO MUCH OF HIS ENERGIES RUING THE PAST, LONG-ING FOR THE PAST, YEARNING FOR THE PAST, REMEMBERING THE PAST, PLANNING ON THE FUTURE, HOPING FOR A BETTER DAY. IN THE MEANTIME THE ONE DAY THAT HE DOES HAVE, THE ONE MOMENT, THE ONLY MOMENT THAT HE EVER WILL HAVE, THE ONLY MOMENT YOU'LL HAVE RIGHT NOW, THE MOST IMPORTANT MOMENT OF YOUR LIFE RIGHT NOW IS THIS MOMENT: SITTING HERE WITH ME, TALKING WITH ME. AND I LIVE THAT WAY, AND IN THAT WAY I HOPE I SHALL LIVE UNTIL I CROAK.

Because our children were living away from home, we thought it sensible to consider living in London full time as neither of us wanted to live the year in Norway, which is where Harry's business was. That summer we found a delightful three-story stucco house on Victoria Road in Kensington. In our front garden was a magnificent 30-foot standard-listed bay tree, and in the back we made a lovely English garden. It was truly our house.

Patrizia carissima,

Visualize, if you can, this moment: mist outside, a vast green-ness of meadow and of woodland, evening, the brook roaring and Mozart's excruciatingly sad slow movement of the *Symphonie Concertante* (violin + violin) and the little house absolutely in order, bowls of wildflowers on each of the tables, Moira asleep on her chair, black-eyed Susans touching the tip of my nose (it is a large nose) as I write; I feel as if I were in some remote corner of Ireland, and yesterday, as I listened to *Tristan and Isolde* from Bayreuth (via telestar), I could hear the shepherd's pipes outside these low windows. I'd company the weekend, and when they'd left, the peace which enveloped this little old house surpassed credulity. Ditto tonight.

I have had your letter and I devoutly hope you've found a house the very sight of which excites you. Otherwise, don't touch it. Wait until the house sets afire something in your soul and you will then know it is *your* house. (That is what happened in this valley in 1958.)

How odd, your reading Sitwell. I've been between *The Scarlet Tree* (Osbert's) and *Taken Care Of* (Edith's). How I love the eccentrics. And I've been rereading *Don't Tell Alfred* (Nancy Mitford) and sobbing inwardly because of the ephemerality of the human condition. All those marvelously eccentric persons: Ottoline, V. Woolf, L. Strachey, E. Waugh, N. Mitford, Carrington, Lawrence, E.M. Forster, T.S. Eliot, Aldous Huxley, etc., etc.—all of them so alive, so alert, so brilliant, so life-loving, so fun-loving, so kind, basically, and humane and capable of deep bottomless laughter: all of them gone, gone, gone. How sad, and yet what a truth the reflection conveys: that transiency is man's chief attribute, and that because of that transiency man should love his brother—share with his brother: and one listens to the news and realizes that those swine who *govern* men and states arrange things so that man hates his brother and kills him. The reflection is enough to make one desirous of solitude and of oneness with trees, birds, hills, clouds, grass, flies, and even the graceful creeping serpents: anything but man (the vandals, the looters, the arsonists, the killers).

Supper was straight out of Athens 2500 years ago: sourdough bread, olives, cheese, onions, wine. And I was rereading *your* V. Woolf as I munched. Since starting this letter there have been two obtrusions *via* telephone: one from a young man wishing to return a horse tonight from Newport, R.I., but the horse's owners are in Georgia, and I'm to do some checking on horse, etc. The other from a dear young girl, a good etcher, whose rich husband fails to give her enough money to run the old farmhouse she occupies with *his* children while he fishes for trout in New Hampshire and for blondes in Sweden. Ah, life—*quelle comédie*!

I am, m'dear, Yours, etc.

John Joseph

John Joseph is referring to The Diary of Virginia Woolf, Vol. I, *which I had sent him in June.*

❦ ❧

19 AUGUST 77
{ TO 12 CHESTERFIELD HILL }
Patrizia carissima,

This will no doubt find you back in London. Here one may with impunity state that glorious fall has set in; splendid blue skies, almost sentimentally rose-colored sunsets, freezing nights. A fire burns this minute and the sun outside is adazzle. Weather such as this makes one euphoric: it is so delicious to breathe. And the greenness of the sunwashed hill is simply astonishing.I have by multitudinous guests been inundated; but I rather like it.

I am in the process of developing a fine art; the art of loafing. But I am rereading *sans cesse*: Turgenev and Trollope particularly, but V. Woolf's Letters, Journals, and Essays are always right on me table. And lots of walking: long walks, I'm delighted to add, usually in the evening, so that by the time I arrive back here owls are hooting lugubriously and katydids are creating one hell of a racket. Last night the temperature was in the low forties when I reached this old Shack. All me love and esteem, etc.,

Yours,
John Joseph

6 AUGUST 78
{ TO 46 VICTORIA ROAD }
Patrizia carissima,

I had guessed, from your prolonged silence, that you must have abandoned Kensington for Norway or for Italy or even for Japan. And there you were indulging in mushroom-hunting and trout fishing. You've escaped the streaming steaming shrieking mobs of American tourists. My local friends, who went for 21 days, returned after 9 days.

I have just read, for the 3rd time, Iris Murdoch's *A Word Child*: an admission which tells alot about me. I really believe Iris to be a witch of some sort; and she sees life for what it is everywhere: i.e., despair, whether "quiet" or *molto agitato*. Hers is the godless, hopeless, joyless, almost meaningless London, which, as you know, is a real place. Then, again, she is powerful in contriving situations and relationships which wrench one when one reads about them. You will be amused to know that this time I had my London sheet-map handy, in order to follow the narrator down the Gloucester Road, across the park into Bayswater, into Lexham Gardens, onto Kensington High Street, and right to T.S. Eliot's church on the Gloucester Road, St. Stephen's. D'you know it? It's a short walk from your house: quite near Cornwall Gardens. Go in and read the memorial tablet which asks one to pray for the repose of the soul of Thomas Stearns Eliot.

Fall is coming. Gathered herbs yesterday. Cold this a.m. Heat on. Have had much company all summer. Have managed a Tanglewood concert (followed by a meal at a French *hostellerie*, where the prices were as absurd as those at Lutèce); and a marvelous production of Turgenev's *A Month in the Country*. And a visit to the exquisite Clark Institute. What a museum!

Do give my best to Harry. Do be aware of your charmed and blessed *modus vivendi*. The world is hurtling towards mass madness. How soothing to learn that there is a remote quiet corner where one can hunt for mushrooms, read, poach trout and breathe clean air.

All me love, etc.

Yours
John Joseph

26 JULY 79
{ TO NESET }
Patrizia carissima,

That "carissima" is no idle epithet, since it has been literally aeons since last I saw you. This will, I hope, find you cool and tranquil among the crays and lingonberries, dutifully arranging pelmets for the west windows of the country house. I was, over the weekend rereading *The Severed Head*, and in that novel the sister of the narrator, Martin, has a thing about pelmets, constantly arranging them for his flat in Lowndes Square. And, by the by, the American Dictionary, Webster's, does not contain "pelmet." How's that for insularity?

D'you recall that morning years ago you phoned and asked if I knew what a pelmet was? I did know, and you were delighted. Well listen to this: it is by H.G. Wells and is addressed to Elizabeth Bowen: "In your next book you may have pelmets in one room but you must not notice them in more than one room. Pelmet is a rare and therefore an arresting word." Q.E.D. And there you have the plebeian's objection to an aristocratic word. I thought, when I read the passage last night, that you would be amused. How many pelmets have you in your London house? The little shack hath them not.

Gardens here are beginning to burgeon, and the zucchini-al pesto season is full upon us. New Zealand spinach, which is really not a spinach, is succulent. Tonight guests from Cape Cod (if they ever get here) are bringing fresh fish, which I shall poach and serve with N.Z. spinach lightly steamed.

I have abandoned my "Memoirs" because Iris Murdoch's *The Sea, The Sea* covered the topic and of course covered it so masterfully that my version of Memoirs emerged a thin and pallid and absurd non-memoir. However, her main character and I have many things in common; an abhorrence of paper napkins, a dependence upon herbs and modest wines, no-nonsense cookery, a delight in solitude, and a continuous profusion of visitors. What I do lack is his nostalgia for his teenage girl whom he finds, in his retirement, a dowdy old thing married to a repulsive creep. I long ago ceased looking for my teenage girl, since, *horrible dictú*, she was the victim of a vicious fire. I was going to work her into my Memoirs somehow, but now all these pages are going to be kindling for a fire the next chilly night we have. All would-be writers should toss into the flames their puny efforts: a few good books might appear.

I have been trying to analyze this Iris Murdoch enthusiasm of mine. Is it my repressed Anglo-mania? My devotion to London and to Oxford (which pop up constantly with Iris)? Is it the pure vigor of her prose? No, I think it is the nightmare world which her characters inhabit. And all those convoluting relationships: They are *partout*! Even 'way up here in the hills. Or should I say particularly up here in the hills? As soon as I seal this, I shall return to the healing waters of my *fons sacra*. Horace had his *fons* Bandusia: I have Shingle Brook . . . Remember, nothing lasts, everything flows, there is meaning nowhere—none whatsoever in that mystery yclept Time.

Con amore,
John Joseph

FROM *Mr. Joseph at Lost Thyme:*

I ALWAYS HAVE BEEN A WRITER, I'VE SPENT ALL OF MY LIFE WRITING. AND I'VE ALWAYS BEEN A SURREPTITIOUS WRITER, I'VE NEVER SHOWED MY WRITING TO ANYBODY AND I'VE NEVER REALLY TRIED TO SELL IT. I STILL WRITE, I SPEND A GREAT DEAL OF TIME HERE WRITING. I WRITE MANY ANECDOTES

FROM MY CHILDHOOD, MANY ANECDOTES THAT HAVE TO DO WITH MY PARENTS, ANECDOTES THAT HAVE TO DO WITH SCHOOL. AND THE PEN FLOWS VERY FLUIDLY, IT FLOWS VERY EASILY, AND THEN I FOLD THEM, I PUT THEM AWAY, AND I LOSE THEM. IF I WERE TO CROAK SUDDENLY AND YOU WERE TO CLEAN UP THIS APARTMENT, YOU WOULD FIND HERE, AND THERE, AND UNDER THAT PILE OF BOOKS AND IN THE BEDROOM, YOU WOULD FIND FOLDED BITS OF PAPER AND THERE WOULD BE THESE ANECDOTES THAT I'D BEEN WRITING. WHEN I FIND THEM I GENERALLY BURN THEM. I JUST WRITE THEM BECAUSE I HAVE GREAT DELIGHT IN WRITING.

Harry had a series of small strokes at Neset and, being a true Norwegian, he had refused at first to see a doctor. My daughter, Siri, and Peik flew over at once, and when they left, Leif came.

8 OCTOBER 79
{ TO 46 VICTORIA ROAD }
Patrizia tristissima,

With Harry I spoke yesterday and he sounded good; exceedingly vigorous and optimistic sans the slightest trace of the valetudinarian's complaints. I believe it to be dismal bad form to interrogate persons who've been sick about their condition; and so I abstained from references to his crises. But how frightening for you. Like you, he applauded and blessed his family. (But what's a family all about anyway if it does not gather when distress signals appear?) He affirmed what I'd suspected; that you are eminently pleased with the house and with the garden.

Fall is here and there are gorgeous spectacles all around one, but nothing compares with the sight of fawns feeding on an adjacent meadow. How do those deer-killers have the savagery it takes to slaughter those lovely creatures? If I had a gun, I should shoot some of the coarse, crass, gross, creeps who flock hitherto during the "open season."

Today's sunlight would dazzle your eyes. But there's a bit of wind. However, only yesterday, I picked a basket of tomatoes, navets, and broccoli. And a bowlful of nasturtiums.

All me love, etc.
John Joseph

28 NOVEMBER 79
{ TO 46 VICTORIA ROAD }
Patrizia carissima,

The fall has been a cornucopia of marvels: warmth, glorious sun, brook-bathing, and the marvel of flocks of geese and of ducks overhead, many of them loitering to forage in the fields of local farmers who have at last harvested their cow-corn. Company galore here: and much activity in the Northhampton-Amherst region. Just fancy how fashionable this neck of bucolic N.E. has become; went to supper at a spot in Northhampton in whose wine-book $150.00 wines were listed. I asked the waiter if we were at Claridge's.

The wood-stove is installed; the wood is piled high; and winter lies lurking with a smirk just beyond the lilac-bushes. Are you seeing much theatre? Lunching downriver at Greenwich? Shopping at Fortnum's? Tea-ing at Claridge's. Reading Margaret Drabble and Muriel Spark? Walking down Gloucester Road?

Con amore,
John Joseph

P.S. A friend, just back from London School of Economics, says he took my advice and read *A Word Child* with a map of London on his desk. A new experience: "geographical-literary," as Polonius would call it.

There's a bookshop in Northhampton yclept The Quill: Very good. And a Scandinavian cafe next door, with excellent "open" sandwiches—just as in Copenhagen. And a shop that sells Stilton and Bath Oliviers. And about a dozen movie-houses and 200 pubs. What a change the Five Colleges have wrought. Now everyone wants to live in this region. So I'm told by a Northhampton barker. And one morning, quite early, a W. Hartford dame that I had not in years seen visited to ask about finding a house in these parts. She is 78 years old and wants to live "where the action is." Lord, help us.

❧ ❧

Harry wrote and privately printed for friends an account called The Last Boat to New York, *about his escape from occupied Norway in the summer of 1940 in a 38-foot sloop. Along with three companions, he had sailed from a small fishing village on the south coast of Norway across the Atlantic to St. John's Newfoundland and then to New York, where they had a hero's reception. The trip had taken them 54 days.*

15 DECEMBER 79
{ TO ARMONK }
My dear Harry,

I have just finished *Last Boat to New York* and want you to know that you should remove yourself from shipping and devote yourself to writing: for you accomplish that all too rarely encountered feat: you tell a story with economy of language, so that the result is a clarity, energy, and excitement. Being, as you know I am, extremely pedantic and trying to be, as you know I do, literary, I read, with something approaching incredulity, your enormously clear prose *via* which you bring that memorable sea-crossing to life. The section I most admire (and I envy you for having experienced it) was that which described the numerous birds near the Faroe Islands. That must have been a thrilling, warming moment on the cruel, cruel sea. I should have been with you. I have cooked on many cruises to and from Maine, and I have never been seasick.

Thanks -

Yours,
John Joseph

✦–✦

In March, Harry and I went to Russia to visit Thomas Watson, the American Ambassador to Russia, who was a friend of ours.

19 APRIL 80
{ TO 46 VICTORIA ROAD }
Patrizia carissima,

Your reaction to the splendours of St. Petersberg; how apt. What, since 1917, have the Russians constructed worth, as Michelin puts it, a détour? Their sputniks and tanks? Their state nurseries and asylums-for-dissidents? I should not, for a wilderness of monkeys, wish to visit Russia: the ironies would kill me. And yet, if one heeds history, is it not the way of the world? Those who built Knole, Blenheim, and all those glorious London churches (Hawksmoor, O my Hawksmoor) have been succeeded by a horde of grubby labor-unionists who will leave behind, as a cultural heritage, ugly Council Housing flats.

I sound like a snob of snobs: and like Virgina Woolf, I say, Yes I am a snob—in the large sense. I yearn to crush no social milieu: I merely think of what man has once achieved and what he is doing today: he's on the point of destroying it all—the art, the architecture, the music, the human element, the guiltless birds and quadrupeds. I am a super-snob: I'd like to secede from the human race when I think of the events of each day. Blacker and blacker the ominous clouds become; and more and more stupid and blind those persons on whom the survival of *all* of us depends. How did the human race allow itself to sink so deeply into the pit?

A cold spring here, but delicious. If only the deities grant me a chance to enjoy rich and enviable solitude for a few years, I shall consider myself blessed beyond words.

Yours apolitically,
John Joseph

P.S. Go to Hatchard's and procure the paperback: *English Parish Churches* by Smith, Cook & Hutton, pub. by Thames & Hudson—what glorious photographs, including our Hawksmoor.

❦- ❧

This is the only letter of mine to escape the flames. I have no idea how it survived.

NESET
31 JULY 1980
John Joseph carissimo,

Have you read the Lyttelton-Hart-Davis Letters? They are a

delight. If you haven't got the two volumes and can't get hold of them let me know and when I return to London in Sept. I will send them to you. They are what letter writing is all about and the fact that George Lyttelton reminds me of you and your letters gives me added pleasure. H-D to L: "Do you know anything about graphology? All I can remember from two expert friends is that when the left-margins of a letter grow wider as they descend, it shows that the writer is moving ever closer to the person he is writing to." (!) Describing the countryside as a "toft and quillet of land" L to H-D: "I shall be with you in spirit among the Pyrenees. Breathe deeply and do nothing at all that you don't like." Pure J.J.! What a treat is in store for you.

I got here one week ago and the weather has now turned whoreson (L-H-D). I am doing alot of writing and reading. As soon as I finish Vol. II of L-H-D I will turn to *Journey for Our Time: The Journals of the Marquis de Coustine* then *Travellers in Europe*— J.G. Lines. If there is any time left I'll start in on books that I have here and that are mentioned in L-H-D.

The garden was a jungle in London due to all the rain. I pruned, weeded, staked and cut out and left it looking the way it should—a tamed wild profusion of roses, clematis, wisteria and other climbers as well as borders with grey, white and blue and in between the flagstones an exuberance of growth.

Please excuse the horrible writing but I must perforce use a drawing pen as *la plume de mon mari est disparue*.

Con amore,
Patrizia

The margins of John Joseph's letters sloped dramatically from left to right. The first line on the top of the page might have nine words and the last on the bottom of the page might have two.

❦ ❧

I stopped at Lost Thyme on my way down from Stowe to Armonk. John Joseph treated me to a splendid lunch of fresh Bibb lettuce, basil, red radishes, and cucumbers from his garden; a perfect soufflé with Gruyère plus Parmesan with chives; a crusty French baguette from the local bakery; and Beaujolais. After lunch we walked along the dirt road in back of the house. I was only there for about three hours, but it was a delightful visit.

11 AUGUST 80
Patrizia carissima,

The letters sound delightful, and as you know, I have ever been one to delve into the letters of others (and into their journals). Nosey, in short; but of how many delightful hours should I have deprived myself all these years were I not nosey. Then again, in letters, writers are, I believe, utterly bereft of disguise, of costume, of posing: in letters, that is, between honest loving friends. How little of the *real* Virginia Woolf we should know, were we bereft of her letters. And how, as Nancy Mitford would put it, "sad-making" that so few persons have the time or the inclination to write letters. With me, I daresay, letter-writing takes the place of cocaine or Irish whiskey—more a vice than an innocuous bit of scriptural dabbling. But what motivates my lust for letter-writing is the vast number of letters that fills my rural box each week.

Today I received a long and charming letter from a former student, now a poet living in Provence, and he speaks of his wife's godfather, Hugh Walpole, whose house in Kensington is full of Duncan Grant paintings and Degas drawings. I believe my friend's wife's family possess the house. And from an utter stranger in San

Francisco, eight pages (!) describing her grief and desolation at the destructiveness and hatreds engulfing us. The young lady says her present "beau" is one of my former students who has allowed her to read my letters to him and from those letters saith she, she feels that I am one who may have some answers. I shall have to dis-illusion the sweet girl and explain that there are ultimately, no answers since ultimately, no one knows what the questions are. Greed, cruelty, hatred; all of them attributes of the human race and who would be so fatuous as to attempt to account for them. If there *be* an answer, it is simply this: the Devil exists and the Devil hath powers: and each of us hath within himself or herself some-thing of the Devil. If I have not bombed the Bologna station, I must partake of the guilt of bombing it since he (or she) was my broth-er or (sister) who bombed it. And though I deplore the outrageous murder of those poor creatures in the 2nd class waiting-room, I deplore too, the malevolent powers that drove my brother or sister to plant the bomb. There now, enough of bombing.

Agreeable tidings; on Saturday I had four eminently civilized guests, three of them Londoners. The weather was bright, dazzling Septemberish, and highly aromatic (mint, monarde, thyme and pine). Off we went, *via* back roads (deeply wooded) to Northhampton and lunched exquisitely in the garden of a Danish restaurant ("Tivoli platter": herring, caviar, ham, beef, hard-cooked eggs, greens, sauces, etc.) and had two bottles of a lovely dry Blanc with lunch. Then off to the Smith College Gallery to see the lovely Degas portraits, the Monets, the Eakins, the J.S. Sargents (a Sargent I'd never before now seen—"The Dining-room" with that atmosphere of comfort and simplicity, with that "unkemptness" which the British have exalted into a fine art), and a heap of Rodin sculptures. Then off to Northhampton's *très chic*

Beardsley's, where I know the barmaid and the five of us sat at the bar while Grushenke (straight out of *Kalamazoo*) served us Bass Ale. Thence to a wine-shop where a couple of cases of wine were acquired; and finally back here, to bathe with lavender soap and luxurious towels in the brook.

My London friends were absolutely overwhelmed—particularly when we stopped in Old Deerfield and looked at some of the splendid old houses there. But O the strange, the enchanting, the life-making air of the day; the September breeze; the promise of golden leaves and of blue sky and of glorious winter snow.

At last you came and visited. You stayed too briefly. You had only a thin sampling of life in these abandoned hills. I must give you such a day as I gave my Londoners. A fond hello to Harry. And forgive the loquacity.

Con amore,
John Joseph

The Bologna train station had been bombed on 2 August 1980 killing 79 and wounding 160 people.

❦ ❧

8 SEPTEMBER 80
{ TO 46 VICTORIA ROAD }
Patrizia carissima,

I have been having an "ecclesiastical" morning, in the strictest sense of "ecclesiasticality," studying the photographs of numerous "ecclesias" in my beloved book *English Parish Churches:* and when I came upon St. Mary Woolworth and the Spitalfields Christ Church, I thought with longing of Nicholas Hawksmoor's work and vowed that err I croaked I should go to Castle Howard and see his Mausoleum there. And I must see the nave (all winged angels) in St. Wendreda, Marsh, Cambridgeshire. Don't you love the name Wendreda? Why an "ecclesiastical" morning should move me to my writing-table to write you in London I cannot explain, though I'm not certain that you should be flattered that the session with lovely churches should remind me of you.

It is autumn this morning, bright dazzling sun with the temperature down to 42 and I have a fire crackling in the stove and have just breakfasted on Darjeeling and toast. The 42 temperature reminds me that I must bring into the house the pots of basil, or I'll have no pesto this winter. In Provence they say "pistou" and they use butter more often than olive oil.

Are you reading the Pym novels? She manages, somehow, in her own quiet unobtrusive way, to create a quite unforgettable canvas: older persons being, alas, as silly and as sorry as older persons usually are. Her *Excellent Women* (v. Jane Austenish) is excellent, and she wrote it back in the 50's. Is there a vogue now in London for Barbara Pym? She's become quite the thing hereabouts. Updike and Iris Murdoch both think highly of her; which means she pleases both ends of the spectrum.

Saw Colleen Dewhurst as Mme. Ranerskaga in *The Cherry Orchard* in Williamstown, and though I went expecting her to slip on the job, she made an unforgettable Ranerskaga—that deep rich cigarette-whiskey voice, which I'm sure the original Ranerskaga must have had. She'd had, after all, what was called (even by her brother) a dissolute life in Paris. Numerous plays and things scheduled for the Amherst-Northhampton area. It never ceases; films, plays, concerts, dance, exhibitions, etc. In fact, there is me fears, a bit too much "Kultur" hereabouts. It's almost too ubiquitous for comfort, though it often is welcome after too much of the bucolic.

My best to Harry.

Yours, etc.

Con amore,

J.J.

❦ ❦

I had written about my travels in Greece with a friend in 1966 and sent the manuscript to John Joseph for his evaluation.

9 SEPTEMBER 80

{ TO 46 VICTORIA ROAD }

Patrizia carissima,

Yesterday, just after posting you an "ecclesiastical" letter, I received your MS. I read it last night; I read it again this morning. It is crisp, uncluttered, vivid, and for me, nostalgic-making. Thanks immensely. Mycenae, the day I visited it, was absolutely bereft of humanity; the sky was grey and those evil mountains glowered, as they must have done on that fateful day when Agamemnon returned from Troy to his darling Clytemnestra. Did you not descend, at Mycenae, into Clytemnestra's Well, a long, long spiraling into the depths with a candle in your hand until you came to the subterranean spring which must have kept the acropolis at Mycenae supplied with water when the enemy besieged it? And at Epidaurus I had a dividend, which you lacked: Maria Callas, singing Norma; and "Ari" Onassis, surrounded by a gang of thugs, arriving just before sunset, which was "curtain time." Your Delphi was my Delphi: but I also had the eagles and a magnificent electric storm, bolts of lightning *under* one, not *above* one. You made a note I made; that Greeks serve their foods lukewarm, so that, at times, the lamb-fat can be seen hardening on the rim of the plate.

I think *nothing* in Greece was so lovely as the olive-groves under Delphi. What a marvel of greenery, soft greenery, after the bony stark landscape up above. I read your essay with my red pencil poised in my best editorial style, ready to pounce on errors. But actually you made only *one* slip, and that the kind of slip which only a sinister old pedant like me would observe. You are saying: "We decide that three bottles of wine a day are too much. We should only have two." The "only" is misplaced. What you mean is this: "We should have only two." But as I have said, I am being obnoxiously pedantic. On the plus side; you write without yielding to the temptation to overwrite; for although your joy and your enthusiasm are high, you keep the prose under control extremely well.

Yours con amore,
John Joseph

This note was attached to my manuscript on Greece.

{ TO VICTORIA ROAD }

Patrizia

Your style, whether you know it or not, is early Hemingway. You maintain a series of severely simple sentences; very few complex sentences; all of which I find vivid and resounding with truth. Your lack of "literary" affectation is refreshing. Here and there, you approach the poetic.

As for your use of "so," read the writers you warmly admire and you will find that they do *not* slip into the habit of transforming the adverb "so" into a conjunction. Syntactically, you may *not* join two independent clauses with the adverb "so" following a comma; it may follow a semi-colon.

Note:

1. It was cold so I wore an overcoat. (Wrong!)
   It was cold, so I wore an overcoat. (Wrong!)
2. It was cold; so I wore an overcoat. (Correct!)
3. It was cold, *and* so I wore an overcoat. (Correct!)
4. It was so cold that I wore an overcoat. (Best!)

Am I not the most meticulous pedant? Please forgive. But you are *not* alone in your abuse of "so." Listen to the politicians' speeches, but read E.B. White (the best prose-writer, I think, of our time) and see whether or not he slips. So!

Très froid here today, with dazzling sun. Fire in the stove. Hot tea as soon as I can make it. "Winter is acoming in, loud hoot owlets."

All me love,
Giovanni Giuseppe

❦—❦

About the same time, I had also sent J. J. my essay on our trip to Russia in March 1980 for critiquing.

6 OCTOBER 80

Patrizia Carissima

Class will be seated and listen to the ancient preceptor.

a. Regarding "split infinitives"; it is bad form (as well as asyntactical) to say "I want you *to truthfully tell* me". One says, "I want you to *tell* me truthfully." (Am I being pedantic? Yes. But you *want* to be guiltless of solecism.)

b.   Regarding "got," "gotten," etc.; "got" and its cousins indicate a poverty of vocabulary. Note this egregiously poor sentence; "When we *got* there we *got* a guide who *got* us a canoe and in that canoe we *got* to the island." The writer is too lazy to say precisely what he means. And so a plethora of "got's."

c.   Regarding the use of "very"; "very" is the Latin "vere," which means "truly". Its use should be severely limited. It's a salesman's word, a seller's word; e.g., "This is a *very* lovely cat." Or "This is a *very* fine house." Don't try to "sell." Now listen and be honest in your reaction:

1.   "He is a wise man."

2.   "He is a very wise man."

The first sentence has more "punch" than the second, for when I omit the "very," I am not striving to "sell" the idea.

d.   Regarding "any" and "some"; they are both indefinites, and one should stringently avoid indefinites. *Note these two sentences:*

1.   "I have no money."

2.   "I don't have any money."

The first sentence is strong, unambiguous, not at all indefinite.

e.   Regarding "persons" and "people"; when one indicates individuals, one uses "persons"; when one indicates racial, social, political, economic groups, one uses "people." *Note these two sentences:*

1.   "There were six persons at my table."

2.   "I love the Irish people."

f.   Regarding "speak" vs. "talk." Here I am being absurdly pedantic. But "to talk" strictly refers to the physical activity of communicating *via* the mouth. Someone unconscious cannot "talk." When I approach a woman and communicate vocally with her I "speak" with her.

g.   Regarding the "dangling participle" (you have one here); the participle in the phrase modifying the subject must allude to the subject. Note well:

1.   *"Hanging* from the rafters, we found Aunt Nell."

2.   "We found Aunt Nell hanging from the rafters."

In 1. "hanging" modifies "we," and we create a repulsive and amusing absurdity; *we* are the suicides!

Thus for the pedantry, Amen.

Now for the essay: you successfully convey the spirit—dull, grey, depressing, dispiriting—of Russia. Bravo! I was exceedingly (not "very") depressed reading sections of your essay. You brought the gigantic squalor and misery of Communism right into my multi-colored valley!

Con Amore,

J.J.

❦—❧

As promised in my letter of July, when I returned to London in September, I sent John Joseph the first two volumes of the (George) Lyttelton- (Rupert) Hart-Davis letters; a "precious cargo" indeed.

4 NOVEMBER 80
{ TO 46 VICTORIA ROAD }
Patrizia carissima,

To thank you for the precious cargo from London, I telephoned you in the country; but the long dolorous unanswered ringing of the telephone bell I took to be a sign that you had fled these vile shores and were now off in Britain shooting grouse or taking long walks in the City. When I describe the cargo as "precious," I understate. Indeed, at 3:00 a.m. today, I was not sure whether to bless or curse you, for I was deep into Vol. I, about finished with it; indeed my titillation surpassed that which Lyttelton describes when books arrive which he not only enjoys but also, as I do, devours. Had I been left alone in 10 Curzon Street, these two books are the ones I should have elected to steal, since I do have the instincts of a biblioclept.

Gem follows gem and at times I have even shouted aloud, "Bravo!", alarming my poor friend Moira. I shouted a "Bravo" at the verdict of Rupert re *Waiting for Godot*, which, when I saw it, I found ugly dull meaningless twaddle full of empty pretension. In fact, I find myself agreeing with George and Rupert on numerous issues, particularly on the issue which involves "literary criticism" and the one which condemns sharply the hollowness of cocktail-parties. Of course, reading these letters will be the undoing of me; for I find myself shifting my empathy constantly from George to Rupert and vice versa. What is distressing is this; that along with the epistolary art have died the gentleness and the wisdom which created such civilized chaps as George and Rupert. I need not add that when I read the verdict of the graphologist regarding the idiosyncratic way of writing (that angle on the left!), I suddenly found myself an ardent believer in graphology.

Have just finished each letter in Vol. VI of V. Woolf's *Letters*; and I find it singularly odd that though George and Rupert make allusions to numerous friends and acquaintances of V.W., neither she nor Leonard is mentioned in Vol. I. And so at last to the words you will recoil from: "Thank you, thank you enormously!" Life *shall* be dull when I have finished with Vol. II.

Me best to Harry and love London for me.

Yours, etc.

John Joseph

P.S. You have no idea how vast is the gratitude I feel to both George and Rupert regarding their comments on G. Manley Hopkins, on whom I have placed a particular crown. In fact, I try to memorize one or another of Hopkins poems now and then. This fall, as I walked under the dazzling golden maples I sang, at the top of me feeble old lungs, "Margaret, are you grieving, Over Goldengrove unleaving!" If passerby there had been, they would have had me carted away as a dotty old eremite. It was the most enchanting Fall that ever I have witnessed. Friends of mine just back from Stowe says the weekend up there was snowy.

J.

6 NOVEMBER 80
{ TO 46 VICTORIA ROAD }
Patrizia carissima,

This a.m. at 2:45, with infinite rue and desolation, I finished the last letter of Volume II. You may reprimand me for having the greedy inclinations of a swine, but when good things like those letters are placed on my table, my appetite knoweth no limits. But, yes, they were aware of Bloomsbury and, though not attracted to it, were not so harsh to it as others of their generation were. I was delighted to learn that each kept a Commonplace Book. I do. And plan to stuff it with gems from the letters. But here's the charm of the book; one becomes a friend of both George and Rupert and of their families (did not you love Comfort?). The huge surprise came early, when Rupert told of being married to Peggy Ashcroft, whom I remember as a girl playing opposite Burgess Meredith on

Broadway in *High Tor* and, more recently, playing the role of Glenda Jackson's mother in *Sunday, Bloody Sunday.*

As you probably—and correctly—assumed, I experienced monumental delight in their discussion of words, in their love of words, in their worship of words. O, I said to myself, these are me own blood-brothers. What a marvelous time Rupert had with all that reading and collating. D'you recall his researches involving Ada Leverson? The friend of O. Wilde who was called the Sphynx? Who *never* deserted Wilde? Well, our little village library has, of all things, a collection of Ada Leverson's novels, everyone of which I've read—with the conviction that the scintillating passages were delicately superimposed by Oscar himself.

But all those visits to Oxford, to Cambridge, to Yorkshire; all those dinners; all those menus, how Rupert must love Iris Murdoch's *A Word Child*, where each item of every meal is carefully recorded. One letter I am copying out to send to my Oxford friend Catherine; it has to do with meeting Catherine's step-mother, recently married to Isaiah Berlin. Lady Berlin I have met at Oxford and have visited her incredible home at Headington. I remember signing the Guest Book there: "Noel Coward" was inscribed a few lines above mine. And then two letters on John Bagley and Iris Murdoch: "his wife Iris Murdoch was there, coruscating, ('coruscating,' the perfect word, from the Latin *coruscare*, 'to flash') but not offensively, with brains. I liked her, and promised to read her new novel, though I know that in three pages I shall be hailing the coastguard." And later; "His wife is Iris Murdoch, whose brow is practically out of sight in the empyrean. I met her in his rooms at New College. A woman in college-rooms in my day would have meant a major explosion."

Con amore, J. J.

Comfort was the wife of Rupert Hart-Davis.

❦ ❧

I had written to John Joseph about going to a lecture given by Angelica Bell at the Metropolitan Museum of Art in which she talked about her family, relatives, and friends with accompanying slides.

22 FEB 81
{ TO 46 VICTORIA ROAD }
Patrizia carissima,

You possess a latent but sinister prowess at sadism: witness your sending me the notice ré Angelica Bell and her lecture at the Museum. I seethed with envy. I had my witches make incantations and pronounce virulent anathemas. You will probably find that in London rodents have ingested your bulbs. See what the incantations did to the skiing? (The little house has been constantly visited by frustrated skiers.) How was Angelica? Having read all of Virginia's *Letters* and *Diaries*, I can tell you a few things about Angelica, who is a friend of my Taos friends. (Oddly enough: what's left of Bloomsbury keeps in touch with Taos.) Bunny, her husband, was old enough to be her father when she married him. But, good Lord, did Virginia love her Quentin! Poor Virginia was looking for the children she never had and actually did not want, and so Vanessa's progeny were more than nephews and nieces.

Have been buried, for the 2nd time in recent years, in Lévi Strauss's *Tristes Tropiques.* I'm afraid I'm about to make a remark of the sort I detest; a remark involving a superlative; for I think *Tristes Tropiques* one of the few major literary works of this century. The French must read like Proust at his best. And what a rich variety of experience Lévi Strauss enjoyed. And how pertinent is each observation he makes, whether it is of a New York street, a Karachi slum, or a near-extinct Amazonian tribe. And what desolation we have achieved with the primitives, who are practically gone. Hélas.

As I told you, methinks, I. Murdoch's *Nuns and Warriors* was a flat, stale, boring failure. Please don't read it; or attempt to read it; it utterly lacks credibility. O, Iris, my Iris, how thou has faded.

Lovely copious rains: brook roaring; grass green in patches; pussy-willows out. In short, all is ready for a formidable blizzard.

Hello to the Gloucester Road.

Yours, etc.
Con amore,
John Joseph

Editor's note:
Quentin Bell was the son of Virginia Woolf's sister Vanessa Bell and Vanessa's husband, Clive Bell. Angelica Bell was the daughter of Vanessa Bell and Vanessa's lover, Duncan Grant. Bunny, Angelica Bell's eventual husband, had also been the lover of Duncan Grant. Complicated.

❦ ❧

As soon as they became available, I sent John Joseph Volume III of the Lyttleton-Hart-Davis Letters.

4 MAY 81
{ TO ARMONK }
Patrizia carissima,

Whatever the opposite of "serendipity" is, I have it; for I would be away on the occasion of your telephoning me from London. However, it is good to learn that you are returning to these barbarous shores soon (that is, if the Irish allow you to leave).

Naturellement, I dove into the Letters at once and consumed them as Rupert used to consume his detective stories. I was enchanted to meet Ruth, but all at once all those rhapsodies he used to write regarding the beauty of the solitudinous Yorkshire moors seemed hollow and fraudulent. How right the French are: *cherchez la femme*. If Comfort is still alive, how cruel, really, the revelation must be. Rupert still lives, does not he? In any case, thanks to you, the other two volumes of the Letters have given immense joy to friends of mine up here. And I have placed in my Common Book, several of the imperishably notable anecdotes.

It hath been an odd spring here: cool, at times cold, at times dazzling; daffodils now blowing in the wind. But the winter was snowless and the spring thus far almost rainless: which means that we shall be a Sahara by July. Boston was a delight; one of my Oxford boys was married in the Harvard Chapel and was so determined that I be present that he came himself in a motor-car to fetch me. I stayed with friends on Beacon Hill (which seethes with Oxonians); and really, Patrizia I'd quite forgotten how lovely Beacon Hill is. A lush word, "lovely," but the Hill is that, and as I was walking up Beacon Street, to a prenuptial dinner-party, arm-in-arm with the London wife of one of my Oxonians, a dear woman stopped us and said, "My, you two look wonderful together!" Thérése, the girl I was accompanying, is a rare beauty indeed; but to include me in the compliment set me up for years. In fact, I've become unbearably pompous since the moment of that overpowering bit of flattery.

Yours, etc.

John Joseph

Ruth was Hart-Davis's mistress, later to be his wife. His Oxford boys were the Choate boys for whom he wrote letters of recommendation to Oxford. To his gratification, they were all accepted by the university.

❦⬥

SHELBURNE

BASTILLE DAY

{ TO 46 VICTORIA ROAD }

Patrizia carissima,

By the time you receive this, you will have had the steep joy of revisiting your garden in Kensington; indeed, I daresay you've been out in the garden toiling away exultantly among your roses and clematis. Is there any activity more *creative* than gardening, which allows one to watch, as it advances, one's creativity? I was out this morning at 5:30 (the grass icy cold) cutting snapdragons, calendulas, cosmos, and ageratum for the table. And last night there was an almost sinfully aromatic *pistou* sauce for the pasta; for the herbs flourish. Try putting a handful of coriander seeds into Earth: watch the promptitude with which they become vigorous plants, ready for salads and sauces.

I am pleased that you enjoyed *The Manticore*, and I think it a literary feat to write a "Jungian" novel without the absurd and obfuscating jargon of the psychologist's couch. I am going slowly with the Rowse book, for, like you, I think a good book should not be gulped down but consumed slowly, every page giving off its flavour. I like very much his "debunking" the neo-proletarians who from genteel origins spring. Be born a proletarian, and you know only too well that there's damned little romance or glory involved. At Choate (and elsewhere) I was vastly vexed (but only seldom amused) to encounter well-born creatures aping the working-classes. And, naturally, the working-classes vigorously object to that hideous condescension. I recall speaking with an extremely bright and candid black student who told me that if ever the day arrived when the Blacks could chop off the heads of Whites, the first heads he'd go after were those attached to the necks of Choate's "liberal" chaps—rich young masters and students who, in "fighting" their families, identified with the blacks to the point of affecting Afro hairdos, and sloppy garb. I like, too, Rowse's condemnation of "top-priority" which politicians give to "material" things. If one lived *via* "material" things alone, O.K., but there are other avenues; and these the politicians (particularly our American politicos) totally ignore. *Soyez sage. Mes amitiés a Harry* —

Con amore,
John Joseph

14 SEPTEMBER 81
{ TO 46 VICTORIA ROAD }
Patrizia carissima, retrovata,

I sit here by the fire (it is a damp Irish morning) rereading *The Voyage Out* and I think of your summer with Virginia Woolf, envying you somewhat the discoveries you must have made and wondering sharply what you ultimately think of Virginia. I recall vividly that day, aeons ago, when I found, in a second-hand shop, the Harcourt edition of *Mrs. Dalloway*. I started at once to read it and was so *stunned* (the only word) by it that I forthwith began rereading it, I have been "rereading" it all my life. I believe that I was a Harvard freshman ('29-'30) when I first discovered that book. One of the effects on me was that the Novel I was writing underwent a bizarre metamorphosis and became a novel involving one day in Cambridge and Harvard Yard. That novel has long since withered, but I recall interludes inspired by Clarissa's walk in London and by Walsh's snooze in Regent's Park, except that my London was Harvard Square and Regent's Park was the Harvard Yard. All I can recall of that precocious work is my description of pigeons on the steps of Widener's and wire-haired terriers ("wooly dogs" in *Mrs. D.*) scurrying under the elms. The "hero" was a Harvard student having a raw, painful, hideously emotional love-affair with a Boston débutante who wanted to be Pavlova: and all he wanted was a Ph.D. in Romance Philology: what a comedy, as I look back on it, but at the time I was grave, correct, philosophically detached, and a writer of *intense* purpose. Now look at me.

By now, *Mrs. D.* has become something of a documentary. Septimus is Virginia herself: Clarissa is the woman Virginia despised because Virginia could not be such a woman (though, secretly, she would have loved being the hostess greeting the Prime Minister at one of her elegant parties). Walsh is an aspect of Leonard, who must himself, have had a life, tempestuous in its own way, like Walsh's, in India. (For Anglo-Indian matrons substitute native Indiennes.) But, in the final analysis, *London* is the heroine: *London* is the life and the force and the tissue of the novel.

Have you not by this time followed Mrs. Dalloway's walk in London? She lived quite close to Westminster Abbey, and her walk, if you follow the pattern, is a delight. Then follow Walsh, and experience further delight: only don't fall asleep on a bench in Regent's Park, for the police may haul you away (as they once did Lady Strachey at Hyde Park Circle—she wasn't napping, she was dizzy) for drunkenness. And if you look into the window of Hatchard's, may you see those ineffably sad, but beautiful lines (I recite 'em all the time): "Fear no more the heat o' the sun/Nor the furious winter's rages;/Thou thy worldly task hast done,/Home art gone, and ta'en thy wages:/Golden lads and girls all must,/As chimney-sweepers, come to dust."

Now you see why of all rivers on this planet I detest the Ouse, why I envy T.S. Eliot (he knew Virginia), why I loathe Ethyl Smith (she bothered Virginia), why I marvel at James Russell Lowell (he was Virginia's godfather), why I wish I knew Richard Kennedy (he was the boy at the Hogarth Press). Enough. You by this time regret that you told me of your summer with Virginia.

Con amore,
John Joseph

Editor's note:
The Ouse is the river in which Virginia Woolf committed suicide by drowning.

❦ ❧

13 OCTOBER 81
TO 46 VICTORIA ROAD
Patrizia carissima,

Is not this a completely repellent aerogramme? As chauvinistic as anything in Sinclair Lewis's wildest satires? If you have been in London long, *hélas:* for the climate has been such as only the inhabitants of Parnussus and of Olympus know; clarity of atmosphere beyond credence. Sundazzle to drive Manley Hopkins mad, and golden leaves falling in all the back country lanes. Since it is the season of the "leaf-freaks," as we call 'em, I have been inundated, and I have just informed a couple from Connecticut that they *may not* visit this day. Just fancy: over the weekend guests came from London, from Beverly Hills, from Washington, from Connecticut, from Boston, not all at once, *Deo gratias*; but some of them wholly unexpected. However, I have survived, and today my girls in Northampton are giving me a "wine-tasting lunch."

The guest from London was extremely grateful to see the sunlight; he said that London has been having grim weather. Ditto Sussex. Am rereading religiously the *Letters* of you know whom and the *Journal* of you know whom, and I repeat that, as with music and with painting, good writing may be "revisited" and "reseen" and "reenjoyed" again and again.

Con amore,

John Joseph

P.S. A little volume of V.S. Prittchett's stories has just appeared. Some good things in it. Bill Cosby's guard dogs almost bit me on my Sunday a.m. walk. If they "get" me, I shall sue for one trillion dollars.

8 NOVEMBER 81
⟨ TO 46 VICTORIA ROAD ⟩
My dear Patrizia,

As vulgar as I believe weather discussions to be I must not neglect to mention the enchanting clarity and warmth of this November day in the hills. All colour faded, the trees humbly naked and handsome (foliage destroys their essential beauty), the woods bereft of birdsong; still it is all enchanting. I have just from a long walk returned; am sipping a bit of Pomerol and nibbling at a biscuit baked in Israel. Later, in the afternoon, I hope to go to Williamstown. Yesterday was *incroyable*; I was invited by the wine merchant in Northampton to join a "tasting" party; it was more an Edwardian picnic than a tasting; *pâtés, fromages, pains* and O what lovely wines and what delicious company (including two Parisians, who were slightly obnoxious, as all Parisians have to be). Came home; found three visitors from Chicago; fed them fettucine with little meat cakes made from ground veal with bulgar.

But last Saturday was straight out of an *Edwardian* notebook: four guests from W. Hartford, who asked me to provide plates, silver, and wineglasses. (I added cloth napkins; I cannot stand paper napkins.) They brought fried chicken wrapped in linen napkins, cucumber sandwiches, anchovy sandwiches, a collection of wines, fruits, cheese, and cakes: after which I took them for a five mile walk down to the Deerfield River, from which walk they almost expired. But O *quelle journée*: the gods have held back on their exquisite days. We are only *just* receiving them.

Two households I know have acquired, *via* London bookdealers, the Lyttelton-Hart-Davis Letters. (*You* deserve royalties).

How good to learn that you are growing devoted to *la vie à Londres.* Lucky you; d'you say prayers of Gratitude, which express your reaction to the Fates who have made possible this delightful life-pattern which is yours? Have you *not yet* found the house in which my V. Woolf was born?

Have just finished a detestable biography of W.S. Maugham: detestable because "Willie" was essentially a detestable creep.

Yours, etc.
John Joseph

P.S. The more I see of the Clark Collection in Williamstown, the more I believe in miracles. That one should find, in that charming town surrounded by those exquisite hills, a *small* museum so richly and so diversely endowed, challenges one's credence. Recently when I was prowling there, two Bronx matrons asked me if I would translate the French which J.S. Sargent had inscribed on one of his paintings: and when I did the two matrons burst into almost ecstatic gratitude, then asked, "You live nearby?" and when I said I did, they almost melted with envy. "Oy, yoy, yoy, you can come here *often* and see all this beauty? And no admission price! Oy, yoy, yoy!" They were marvelous. I almost took them to the British Maid for a pub lunch. But they were going to prowl the musée till closing time.

Yours,

J.

THE DEATH OF APRIL OF 82
{ TO 46 VICTORIA ROAD }
Patrizia carissima,

How singularly odd: *The London Review of Books* arrives carrying an advertisement for the new Lyttelton-Hart-Davis volume; and your letter arrives, informing me that you have already sent me the volume. Who dares state that there's not a Divinity that arranges such things? Copious thoughts of gratitude and of expectation from Lost Thyme.

The morning is fresh, cool, sunny, aromatic—what a morning. Yesterday we did much cleaning and landscaping here. I've developed a new identity: that of Lancelot "Capability" Brown. Seeing that my wee property has "capability" I am removing and pruning and eliminating, and a miniature English "park" is emerging; not quite another Blenheim, but a "park" to fit the size of this exiguous 18th century cottage. And I've cut more land for flowers and herbs.

Though it has been a "cruel" April (T.S.E. was *so* right), I've seen the following abloom: Hepatica, trillium, bluet, violet, bloodroot. Daffodils and narcissi toss by the stream, which is pellucid and turgid, and what music can touch the minor-key windmoan high in the hemlocks, with a warbler or two issuing liquid accompaniment.

I've spoken with Kathleen O'Hara (Peik's friend) about Rikk's appearance on the Choate platform, and she and I may go down— only for the Rikk Larsen part of the Reunion festivities. So unless a snag arises, I, at your inspiration, tread once again on the holy soil of academia. Kathleen, by the way, has had a cookery book published. In it is *"Pâté de la Maison de Lost Thyme,"* one of my "house recipes."

Saw a lovely film the other evening: *Tre Fratelli*, most touching: and an effective commentary on northern Italy and its terrorist problem. But O the lovely Italian countryside and what a splendid performance by Charles Varel, who is 89 years old and French. It had me as close to lachrymosity as ever I have been.

The Gilbert and Sullivan war in the frigid storm-tossed So. Atlantic keeps threatening. Have the British gone Chinese? "Saving-face." They've absolutely nowt else via which to explain their bizarre but tormenting behaviour. If it were not absolutely sick-making, the whole expedition to the desolate Falklands would be laugh-making. Actually it's Britain's version of Athens' Sicilian expedition: after which the power of Athens was gone. Ditto Britain. Don't they read Greek history at Oxford anymore? Athens in its death throes: Britain in its: two senseless expeditions. And we had ours here: Vietnam. And may soon have another: El Salvador. And to think that Thucydides wrote his *History* to show man how to avoid idiotic international wars. What bloody fools these politicians be.

Con amore,
John Joseph

John Joseph had received the Choate Reunion folder listing the activities planned for their annual reunion. These included a panel entitled "Sunday Symposium: Education and the Arts." Rikk '65, who at the time was a feature-film producer, was invited to participate along with Roger Stevens '29, theatrical producer; Richard McKee '60, opera singer; and Glenn Close '65, actor.

❦ ❦

8 MAY OF 82
{ TO 46 VICTORIA ROAD }
Patrizia carissima,

How adroitly you timed the arrival of Volume IV. I had been to Green Street in Northampton, where I'd found Fortnum's teas and currant jam and marmalade; returned and lo, in the open rural box, a parcel from your favorite bookshop. I need not add that I was immensely impatient to sink into it; and when at length I did, I experienced a curious but delectable psychological phenomenon: not *déjà vu*, but *les amis retrouvés*. Thanks from this quarter are as immense as my impatience and my delight. (My, but Rupert's wife was civilized, sending for Ruth when Rupert was sick: perhaps not so much civilized as clever, for Ruth had to—was glad to, I'm sure—do all the nursing.) Don't you love the food-consciousness of both George and Rupert? And are not some of the "simple"—even frugal—meals exquisitely delicious? At least they sound so.

I thought of you on Friday evening, a lovely balmy spring (Appalachian Spring) evening, when I went down to a *vernissage* in

Amherst: the oils by a friend of mine, the photographs by a Hampshire photography-instructor, the collages by a female apparently having a passionate involvement with adobe houses in the Pueblo county. What made the evening slightly astonishing was the presence there of many young persons from these hills; painters, poets, professors, musicians; they turned my hoary old head somewhat, for all of the young females involved rushed up to embrace and to kiss this antiquated relic. I relished every moment of it, particularly when a young painter came up to me and said, "How come, Joseph, all this affection?" I said something about the girls' awareness of quality when they saw it. Seriously, Patrizia, it was a delightful evening, even though I resisted the champagne, the red and white wine, the mound of plates containing delicacies. For a bucolic backwater, the evening had all the finish and glitter of an evening at a gallery on 52nd St., or better still, on Bond Street.

My "Capability" Brown landscaping is proceding slowly, but visitors comment on the "improvement." Still too cold at night for the garden. A marvelous year for simultaneity of blossoming; because of the bizarre weather, the hepatica, trillium, anemone, violet, bluet, and saxifrage made a début on the same hour. The exquisite polygala will appear next week.

Con amore,
John Joseph

The "favorite bookshop" was Heywood Hill Ltd. The managing director, John Saumerez-Smith, would tell me whenever another volume of the letters was expected and that he would save one copy for me and one for "John Joseph of Lost Thyme."

❧— ❧

{ TO 46 VICTORIA ROAD }
Patrizia carissima,

The News is on the FM and it sickens me deeply to hear bulletins read ré the silly adventure in the South Atlantic. That hysterical woman from Ten Downing Street is often on the FM here and she has, I am certain, blood gushing from her fangs; for blood is awash on those useless rocks called Falklands and before it, the adventure, is over, much blood shall have been spilled. I look about me at Nature's grand effulgence; I listen to warblers chanting on the shrubbery; I smell the grass smells and the pine-smells; then I read the *Times* or listen to the FM, and I grow sick. And that woman shrieks, and I vomit. When I learn that the Britons are largely on *her* side, I realize that the Britons, aware of being located at the darkest corner of the abysm, know that soon, too soon, they will be absolutely finished. If only the British had not given up Greek and Latin, they would have read all about the Falklands in Thucydides, who described Athens's version of the Falklands in his narration of the silly and the destructive Sicilian Expedition. Americans, who read nowt, had their Sicilian Expedition in Vietnam. And Reagan, who is illiterate, will have us another Sicilian Expedition in Central America unless the Fates intervene.

What you tell me of Hart-Davis is illuminating. Who is his present Lady? The Letters (Vol. IV) inspired me to reread Francis Iles (*Before the Fact* and *Malice Aforethought*) who had a talent with murder-stories which are *not* murder mysteries. And, d'you know, Patrizia, I recall reading Iles when he first appeared—50 years ago! When a man speaks of a book encountered 50 years ago, it is time for that man to rush into Brooks Brothers and have himself measured for a shroud.

The gigantic *Candelabrum Primulas* bloom flamboyantly in the flood-plain of my brook, everyone of them a runaway from Lost Thyme. And the "Capability" Brown goes on. (A *pâté* I regularly make was the first course here at supper on Thursday; and me guests gobbled it down with a bit of chilled Orvieto.) I write too much. Forgive, if you can.

Con amore,
John Joseph

P.S. Just returned from my little woodland, where I rediscovered fully abloom the loveliest orchid I know, the *Orens Spectabilis*. It had not bloomed for three years and there were eleven abloom. I was almost out of my mind with excitement.

J.

❧ ❧

I had written John Joseph how, in the hospital after a brain stem stroke, Harry couldn't concentrate when I read to him, but he perked up when I told him that the hummingbird, which had been visiting our terrace every day, was feeding on the flowers. Two weeks after his stroke, Harry's condition began to deteriorate rapidly. He opened his eyes once to Peik and me, and then he went into a deep coma. The next day he died of a ruptured stomach ulcer.

3 AUGUST 82
{ TO ARMONK }
Patrizia carissima,

There are times when the most eloquent language is silence. And such a time is this, the day of Harry's release from anguish and indignity. My mother had an aphorism: "There are many things worse than death." And one of those "things" was that hideous condition of helplessness, speechlessness, and utter dependence. Harry, who *cannot* die so long as you and the children have him in your minds, would agree with my mother utterly. And whatever one says emerges hollow, meaningless, absurd. And so I'll yield to brevity and say that Harry is very much alive and will be forever for you and the children. Look: I was a mere stranger to Harry, and his death has hit me hard, for I doubt that I ever shall meet a man of Harry's quintessential quality—his *gentleness*; and yet he is, and shall be, very much alive for me.

Bless the children for rushing to you. And be grateful for that inner strength which has, before this tragic day, rushed to your aid. When my father (like Harry, a gentle person) died, my mother told us, her brood: "Look, this is not time for grief, but for thanking the Deity for allowing us to share your father's life."

No time for grief. Time for thanking. How right.

Con amore,
John Joseph

❀- ❀

I decided to bury Harry at Neset under the birch tree in the courtyard. My daughter, Siri, and I took him on his final Concorde flight, during which I surreptitiously poured champagne onto the box containing the can with his ashes. I wrote an account of Harry's burial for the family and also sent it to John Joseph.

At Neset I couldn't face transferring the ashes into a more aesthetic receptacle than the can, which carried a sticker warning that it was not rust proof, so I decided to make a collage on the can of momentos from Harry's life, which I could find at Neset.

The next problem was to find a container in which to put the can. The ice bucket from Vaastuen seemed appropriate, but it was too small. Then, Jennie, the cook, produced an identical but larger one. I had bought them both in Copenhagen a few years previously, and the ice bucket had since been chosen by the Museum of Modern Art to be in their permanent design collection. I wondered what Jennie was thinking when she saw a collage on the can of ashes! And to bury the ship owner in an ice bucket! But, as Siri pointed out, Jennie was now an accomplice having found the second ice bucket and also having steamed off the Larsen label from the cognac bottle, which was part of the collage.

I put the can, which now looked festive, in the ice bucket and placed around it a tie painted with tankers and the Gotaas logo; a 1942 Christmas card from the Norwegian Shipping and Trade Mission; one of Harry's winning track metals; a piece of birch bark from one of the birches Harry had so constantly pruned; and my farewell note. Then we sealed it with dripped candle tallow.

It was a clear, sparkling day, the kind of day Peik had characterized many years earlier: "A great day in Norway is better than anywhere else!" Before putting the ice bucket containing the ashes into the hole, Siri and I both kissed it, and after a few shovelfuls, we sprinkled the earth liberally with Larsen Grande Fine Cognac, which Harry liked to tell people was his own company. We found a stone, diamond-shaped like the Irgens Larsen logo and placed it on his grave. Below the stone there was a profusion of bluebells, the flowers that Harry and I had picked when we first came to Neset in 1955.

"En del av mig blir igjen paa tunet" (Part of me always remains in the courtyard) Esben had written in the summer of 1973, and I thought that it was just what Harry would feel, surrounded by his *gamle solvidde gresstekte hus som lukker sig om det vakre tun* (old grass-roofed houses, burnt by the sun, which enclose the lovely courtyard).

❦-❦

9 SEPTEMBER 82
{ TO NESET }
Patrizia tristissima,

What a beautiful ritual you and Siri arranged for Harry. You think he approved? No, my dear, he was profoundly grateful and proud; and that murmur you heard in the birch-tree was Harry's delighted approval. You and Siri thought it was a compassionate sibilant wind; it was Harry himself. And as long as you and the children and the grandchildren have recollection of Harry, so long will he exist as a living and a loving force, albeit to the mortal eye he be invisible. What an enviable final resting-place; for Harry no repellent avenue of graveyard monuments, hideous, outrageous and vulgar in their massiveness, even more hideous in their meaninglessness. I love the liberal sprinkling of cognac—straight out of Greek and Roman ritual, where wine was usually "liberally sprinkled"; and cognac, after all, is simply wine that has been boiled. Harry twinkled at the cognac bit, and he did not say, as a Yankee would say (or, especially, a Frenchman): what a waste.

Now as for being alone, you are being fatuous; for you are not, you cannot be, alone. Too many human beings are involved in your daily life; particularly, those admirable children and those beautiful grandchildren. That wise old woman, Mary Joseph, loved her ten-year period of "aloneness," though, like me, she neither knew or aspired to pure solitude. She used to say, "One must grow used to being alone; for 'aloneness' is one's natural condition." She'd had ten children, 33 grandchildren, and an enormous number of great-grandchildren, but on the last Christmas of her life, at dinner which she shared with me alone, she said to me; "How wise you've been, my son. You've been developing a taste for 'aloneness' and you are not afraid of it." Nor am I. Then she sipped the champagne we'd had with dinner. And she gave me a broad glad wink, repeating, "You're the wise one." Eleven days later, while she slept, the "Angel of Death" (her euphemism for dying) came to fetch her—an answer to her nightly prayer, which concluded with the words "... and may I be spared the indignity of the bedpan." And so was Harry spared. And I pray, selfishly, that I too may be spared.

D'you proceed to London from Norway? or to Cambridge? or where? On the other hand, *qui sait?* That powerful force Naseeb ever plays its hand.

Con amore,

John Joseph

P.S. Did you murmur, as you sprinkled the cognac, *"Ave atque vale"*? Catullus did.

❦ ❧

Shortly after Harry's death, I and the children found out that Harry's managing director and partner in Irgens Larsen was a scoundrel who was planning to take our company away from us.

{ TO 46 VICTORIA ROAD }

My dear Patrizia,

Telephoned East 77th Street and learned, from the Admirable Wong, that you are in London. But I suspect that you may be in Oslo, in the midst of hideous and infuriating litigation, from which I devoutly hope that you will emerge triumphant. I think, with a shudder, of Harry's being victim of the cunning of a scoundrel whom he implicitly trusted. Whom, in this parlous world, can one trust?

Winter, or a foretaste of it, has arrived; and a dour and biting frost has taken my "Giverny" and demolished it. But it is the way of Nature, and living in the depths of the country, one soon learns to see Nature as neither cruel nor benign, but sublimely indifferent. Nature couldn't be the least bit concerned with the blossoms which fed my swelling pride. Have found an early Robertson Davies, *A Mixture of Frailties*, which if you cannot find it among London's Penguins, I'll send you. As I was breakfasting, the FM was playing, as it is wont, "early" music: and when the Aria was completed, the announcer informed us that its title, translated, was "May the Intestines be so Cleaned." I lost me appetite.

I must say you sounded hale and vigorous over the phone. Keep vigorous. And fight mercilessly this rogue who's come into your and the children's life. And, as St. Paul once put it, "Study to be serene." He did not mean "Study *in order to be* serene" but "Study *how to be* serene." Good advice. And last night, while reading Thos. de Quincey on Charles Lloyd, I came upon the following memorable bit: "Put not your trust in any fabric of happiness that has its root in man or the children of man." Tersely, trust no one. Wisdom; not cynicism—when one considers the world we inhabit.

Con amore,
John Joseph

❦–❧

I went to a spa in England called "Forest Mere" to rest from the exhaustion of dealing with the complications of settling Harry's business, and then on to a pheasant "shoot" with friends who lived in Scotland.

8 NOVEMBER 82
{ TO 46 VICTORIA ROAD }
Patrizia carissima,

Delighted but not surprised to hear that Iago's petard backfired. Bravo for Rikk and brava for you: what a formidable pair of opponents you must have been. And now for much-needed rest: benefit from it. As for the shooting-party in Scotland, I've just finished my 2nd reading of *The Shooting Party*, which I think a minor masterwork. What a social document, really, that book is: and full of ironies. I do hope that your shooting-party in Scotland will expose you to no Philistine bores, to no myopic aristocrats. I love non-myopic aristocrats, but those who wear coloured-glasses in order to avoid confronting truth are sad. Only yesterday I was writing about myopic aristocrats when I was describing Carrington's suicide in a letter to a friend terribly interested in Carrington's enigmatic career. I told her that Guinness (Nancy Mitford's brother-in-law) demonstrated what I term "aristocratic myopia" when he lent suicide-obsessed Carrington a gun "to shoot rabbits."

I breakfasted at 5:00 this a.m. (it is now 7:00) and was enchanted to see break over the eastern ridge a rosy-fingered dawn straight out of Homer. And O the peace of this valley at 5:00

a.m. A narrowly circumscribed life, one will say: but it enchants me. And a glimpse of the Great World and its ailments makes me lust after *no* travel.

I have a new cookery "thing": I make "Scotch eggs"—as good, I think as any you may find at one of those Jermyn Street pubs. Having discovered an old-fashioned butcher, I have him grind sausage, cut meats (O his filets!), and describe sauces with me, for he is an amateur Bocuse himself and is good at wine-talk.

Take care of Patrizia and remember always to grasp the *present* moment, to clutch at it, aware that it is the only moment you can trust. I now go off to be interviewed at the local college; a job I shall relentlessly reject—teaching Greek culture and escorting the class to Greece.

Con amore,
John Joseph

12 NOVEMBER 82
{ TO 46 VICTORIA ROAD }
Patrizia carissima,

Page 2 of your last letter is a sheet of notepaper from *Forest Mere* at Liphook in Hampshire. When I saw the words *Forest Mere*, I asked myself why they *seemed* familiar to me. I went about tormented with perplexity for a while until—ah, I recalled! And you, *sans doute, knew* all the time. Evelyn Waugh, in his 60th year, when, through inactivity, excessive gin-drinking, and melancholy, he was extremely *low,* the Ian Flemings urged him to try a "hydro," Forest Mere. Eventually he went, and wrote to Ann Fleming: "You did not prepare me for the great ugliness of house, furniture and scenery here. But my 50 guinea suite is spacious and the attendants civil....In the last 24 hours I have had 2 glasses of hot lemon juice. I have sat in a 'sweat-bath' and been severely massaged. I have gained 1/2 pound in weight. Time hangs heavy." And later: "Did female patient at Forest Mere who took me for a woman observe me in the 'treatment room'? If so, she must be ignorant of anatomy." Tell me: did you encounter the ghost of Evelyn there: or of Ian Fleming? And are the furnishings still ugly? And is the word "hydro" still used? Did it do you much good? All that yogurt would not hurt but would the absence of wine help?

This letter may find you back in Manhattan. How was the shoot in Scotland? And the garden in Kensington? For about a week I have been *sans* motor-car, and d'you know, the absence of a motor-car creates a sense of freedom, quite delicious. I need not add that I have been walking even more widely than formerly. Even walked all the way back from Greenfield College. It was an enormously long walk and two days of inactivity followed, though there was much to do here. *Soyez sereine.*

Con amore, Yours, etc.

John Joseph

❦ ❦

In 1970 I was asked to become a member of the International Council of the Museum of Modern Art, "MoMA," which offered many intriguing experiences, about which, of course, I wrote John Joseph.

23 MAY 83
{ TO 46 VICTORIA ROAD }
Patrizia carissima,

And there you were visiting palazzos in quest of art for MoMA and dining with princes and potentates. Good for you. And what was I doing? Being a "best man" (at me advanced years) at a garden-wedding in Amherst: and being "godpa" to a sweet little girl in Conway: and squiring Mme. Dubonnet (d'you know her?). An American woman, the *last* of the "repatriates," a friend of the Gerald Murphys and of the MacLeishes (whom she adored—both clans) and of Scott and Zelda (whom she loathed, both of 'em). I took her to the deep dark dank forest where Archie MacLeish sleepeth his last sleep, and she was deeply moved and ever more deeply grateful. (Have I told you all this? Suddenly it takes on the tone of déjà-vu.) Then a triad of French-speakers for lunch one day last week on what was *the* splendid day of spring; zephyrs, aromatic lilacs, wild orchids, lambs and heifers, a long walk, a lovely lunch with modest vino. Then to a poetry-reading given by one of my adopted granddaughters at Amherst, and it was a success. (My, my, what *cerebral* persons live in these western Massachusetts towns.)

My Oxford family sent me four thrillers by Colin Dexter, the man who is writing intelligent thrillers these days, whose work takes place in non-academic Oxford. If, like me, you enjoy reading thrillers on weekends, look him up. (Pan Books) I've been reading again Baring's letters to Juliet Duff, and I've been howling with glee. Lord, they're funny. and, naturally enough, some of his poems are literal translations of Horace's odes, which he and Belloc worshipped.

No seedlings in the earth yet: too cold. 26 F. last week, and all the ferns blackened. A warm winter, a cold spring: Nature setting, as she invariably does, a balance. And to us, poor puny creatures, Nature is, as she ought to be, grandly indifferent.

Con amore,
John Joseph

Baring's letters to Juliet Duff are collected in Dear Animated Bust: Letters to Lady Juliet Duff.

❦

6 JULY 83
{ TO 46 VICTORIA ROAD }
Patrizia carissima,

Mal' occhio! I did not sleep last night. Vol. V (bless you) kept me up all night. The saga of Rupert's gathering treasures for the London Library Auction is a most exhilarating bit. How marvelously generous all those literary giants were. See: it proves my point: those who give their lives to *humane* pursuits (writing, painting, music, etc.) are themselves abundantly *humane.* (Can anyone equal Lyttelton's own instinct for humaneness: and he was only a teacher!) How does one thank you for such a splendid gift?

This little "estate" looks madly good. Lawns are as velvety as any along the Loire. My little orchard, planted this spring, looks like a medieval woodcut. The herbs flourish (and *pistou* sauces on everything). The flowers are becoming ostentatious, as flowers tend, wicked vain creatures, to do after heat and rain. And company galore: with some good cooking (modesty does not become me) and some noble wines at table: and an abundance of garlicke.

I've read a couple of reviews (of Iris Murdoch's novel) which do *not* give the novel the black mark it deserves: which simply demonstrates that reviewers do *not* read the books they presume to criticize. Iris will have a tough time reaching such an abysmal level in the future. Bottomless pits do have bottoms; and Iris has reached one.

Con amore, etc.

John Joseph

Iris Murdoch's novel was The Philosopher's Pupil (1983).

❦⟶

Patrizia carissima,

Bizarre: mail from London arrives here more promptly than mail from Boston. That is the sort of bizarrie I like. And what an enchanting garden—with all that rich rosemary, which I should be snitching constantly for lamb. Yes: I know Vita's book on gardens, and I think the most useful bit of information involves tossing into one's flower-garden one's dishwater—or was it laundry-water? Whichever it was, it made for one of the most productive flowerbeds that Vita ever saw. (My dishwater goes into my bed of snapdragons, and Lord, do they love it.)

As for B.B. [Bernard Berenson, art dealer], he does not belong to the list of humane creatures. He was a money-maker. He used his art-expertise and charged creatures like Mrs. Jack Gardner the earth when he procured pictures for them. He was primarily interested in $ $ and in material possessions. The sole humane act of his life came when he left this life: leaving I Tatti to Harvard.

Poor Cyril C. [Connally, author] suffered all his life from being as ugly as a toad. (Even Lady Ottoline's photographs show him to be a repulsive Oxonian undergraduate.) (Remember V. Woolf's malicious comment on him when she found him to be a guest at Eliz. Bowen's Irish house, Bowen Court? If memory serves, V. likened him to an ape.) Actually, there is humaneness in *The Unquiet Grave* and when he ran *Horizon*, he was good to the young unpublished writer. And in *The Evening Colonnade* there are pieces which reveal the toad's humaneness, civility, and charm. As for poor old alcoholic Evelyn, his excessive snobbery was his undoing. His nastiness was his endeavor to battle with his insecurity. But *A Handful of Dust* is the work of a man with a heart and warmth. He became particularly bitter after his wife Evelyn allowed him to be cuckolded. Had he been a sage Italian, he'd have reacted by going out to indulge in a bit of cuckolding himself.

As for the irony of finding yourself the non-owner of Neset, remember my admonition to 40 years of classes: the only Law that prevails is the Law of Irony. One inevitably learns the truth of that admonition if one lives long enough. So simply sneer smilingly: recall that you don't have to worry about its upkeep, its security, and its taxes. (The Russians are destined to grab it anyway.)

Have you read James Fox's *White Mischief*? Don't. (Cyril C. had hoped to write it. But death caught up with him.)

Con amore, etc.

John Joseph

P.S. On Tuesday I met, on me road, a black bear that was easily the most immense quadruped that ever I did see outside a zoological Park. He altogether snubbed me, making me feel like a "second-class" citizen—which, I know, I am.

J.

I was the non-owner of Neset because I had had to sell it, but the friend who'd bought it included in the bill of sale that I would have the right to use it for two months during the summer for as long as I lived.

Editor's note:
Evelyn Waugh's wife was also named Evelyn.

14 SEPTEMBER OF '83
{ TO 46 VICTORIA ROAD }
Patrizia carissima,

How exquisite you make Norway's climate appear; here we've had nowt but intense heat with heavy mugginess—the climate of Calcutta or of D.C. Whoever (I think it was Sam. Johnson) suggested that weather is a topic to be avoided in conversation and in letter-writing must have been myopic, for how can one pretend to ignore the stupendous fact of *climate*? Of late persons in this area have had frayed nerves because of the unwonted humidity, and on some days it was deadly attempting to walk: the sun can be sinister as a bear or a tornado. But, *Déo gratias*, for three days now we've been having a touch of fall, that most gracious and civilized of seasons. Now in London you must be busily doing theatre, film, gallery, ballet, and gastronomy.

Can you believe that I have been re-reading the George-Rupert Letters? How copiously supplied they are with anecdotes. One may create a tremendously exciting book of "Extracts" from the Letters, merely presenting anecdote after anecdote. I have dined out on the incredibly funny anecdote regarding W.S. Maugham's recipe for a successful short-story which he gave to a girl's school. D'you recall it? W.S.M. said a good short story should have among its ingredients a bit of mystery, a bit of religion, a bit of sex, aristocratic characters and plain language. And when the girls endeavored to write a short story meeting W.S.M.'s requirements, one bright child created what must be the most terse and successful short story in English: "God!" yelled the Duchess, "I'm pregnant again! Who done it?" or words to that effect. I told the story down on Cape Cod. My listeners howled with glee. So thank you.

Yours, etc.

J.J.

❦

In January 1984 John Joseph called me at Cambridge, MA, and read me the following letter from Rupert Hart-Davis. He was both excited and mystified. He said that he must have written a letter to Rupert Hart-Davis and forgotten writing it among all the other letters he wrote. He had decided the letter was a hoax sent to him by his Oxford friends, but they had denied it. I told him that, if he'd send me a Xerox copy of the letter, I'd show it to John Saumerez-Smith, manager of my favorite bookstore in London, who could authenticate it. John Joseph died before I was able to do this. What pleasure he would have gotten to learn that it was from Hart-Davis.

3 AUGUST 83
THE OLD RECTORY
MARSKE-IN-SWALEDALE
RICHMOND
NORTH YORKSHIRE

My dear John Joseph,

Ever so many thanks for your lovely letter which arrived this morning, and has given me enormous pleasure. I'm so glad you have enjoyed those books: how did you hear of them, I wonder? The sixth and final volume is due to appear next March or April.

In 1964, after eighteen years of waiting, my beloved Ruth and I were able to marry. I retired from publishing, we found this lovely old house in our favorite dale, and lived here blissfully until

31 January 1967, when Ruth died of a heart attack, in a split second, without illness, pain, knowledge or fear. A wonderful way to go, but for me, it was the end of the world. But I gradually recovered, largely due to my present wife, June—a much younger friend of mine and Ruth's—who is an angel of goodness and spoils me outrageously. So you see, I am really an extremely lucky old man.

Since 1963 I have written, edited, or compiled twenty books. The next one to appear will be a selection from my commonplace book called *A Beggar in Purple*, which Hamish Hamilton is to publish on August 25. I think perhaps you might like it. Thank you again for writing.

Yours gratefully,
Rupert Hart-Davis

P.S. My letter slopes to the right almost as much as yours. Graphologists say this means that you're leaning towards the person you're writing to. So be it.

29 FEBRUARY 84
{ TO 46 VICTORIA ROAD }
Patrizia carissima,

After almost two weeks of exquisite spring, winter, with vicious vengeance, hath returned: sleet, ice, snow, ferocious winds, and me poor little snowdrops, which were blooming on the south side of me little shack, are now buried, but if you're going to call yourself a "snowdrop," what're a few inches of snow?

I have tried several times to reach you *via* telephone, but the "circuits are busy." I wished to tell you that a neighbour lent me an immense book containing many of Maurice Baring's writings,

at right, JOHN JOSEPH'S LETTER OF 29 FEBRUARY 84

29 february 84

Patrizia carissima,

After almost two weeks of exquisite spring, Winter, with
vicious vengeance, hath returned: sleet, ice, snow, ferocious winds,
+ me poor little snowdrops, which were blooming on the south side of
me little shack, are now buried, but if you're going to call yourself
a 'snowdrop', what's a few inches of snow?... I have tried several
times to reach you via telephone, but the circuits are busy? I wished to
tell you that a neighbour lent me an immense book, containing many
of Maurice Baring's writings, including that wonderfully 'dated' novel,
The Lovely Lady of Dulwich. I wanted, too, to suggest that you
pick up Anthony Powell's _To Keep the Ball Rolling_ (a Penguin),
in which all of our old literary pals appear, particularly
Hart-Davis + Ruth! (I'm certain you've already read the
book: you're always three steps ahead of me.)... D'you know
the Irish writer, Molly Keane? I've been lost in her
Good Behaviour, very Irish, very sad-funny (as only Irish
writers can be). I'm told that her 2nd novel is even
better than _Good Behaviour_. It appears that after 30
lazy years she has begun to write. In the '30's
she was quite a figure, writing under the name
'M. J. Farrell.' She thinks she'll please you. (But, again,
you've already read her?)... And Geoffrey
Madan's _Notebooks_ contains aphorisms worth
reading, particularly those in French...Still
doing Italian poems. This fragment from
Quasimodo is, I think, a gem:

Non sa la morte mentre muore
il canto chiuso del divo, tanta intorno
la sua caccia d'amore, continua
un arco aperto, rivela la sua
solitudine. Qualcuno verrà.

Your Italian is up to translating it.
Con amore, etc
John Swope

including that wonderfully "dated" novel, *The Lovely Lady of Dulwich*. I wanted, too, to suggest that you pick up Anthony Powell's *To Keep the Ball Rolling* (a Penquin), in which all of our old literary pals appear, particularly *Hart-Davis and Ruth*! (I'm certain you've already read the book; you're always three steps ahead of me.)

D'you know the Irish writer Molly Keane? I've been lent her *Good Behavior*. It appears that after 30 long years she has begun to write. In the '30's she was quite a figure, writing under the name of "M.J. Farrell." Methinks she'll please you.

Con amore, etc.

John Joseph

15 MARCH 84

{ TO 46 VICTORIA ROAD }

Patrizia carissima,

And once again London, where no doubt daffodils and snow-drops and crocuses abound. Here it has been a bizarre spell of spring weather: excessively high temperatures, swiftly melting snows, and now incessant rains. And what with *The Transit of Venus* (Shirley Hazzard) and *The Black Prince* (Iris Murdoch) and several other tomes, including a fascinating archeological work of Silbury Hill down near Avebury, I am a bit vertiginous.

The Black Prince is tumultuous (almost a bit "too much"), *The Transit of Venus* is beautifully chiseled, and most cunningly put together, with vast economy. But both novels are much preoccu-pied, or obsessed with the idea of Love. Good Lord! If only "Classical education" were restored, we'd have all the answers, for who needs clarification after meeting Helen, Andromache, Hecuba, Medea, Penelope, Phaedra, Dido, Cleopatra, Catullus's

Clodia et al.? Just fancy: I've now erected a case in favour of a Classical training for I vehemently believe that all the questions of Love are asked and answered in Classical Literature. How do readers escape Plato's *Symposium*? Iris's characters in *The Black Prince* are all totally *non compos mentis* regarding Love. (What's Iris's marriage like? Since she's often writing from the male's point of view, she may be androgynous, in which case her marriage, like that of two other celebrated androgynes, V. Woolf and J. Joyce, is secure. Is that why divorce is ubiquitous: not enough androgynes?)

Had a cold. The local M.D. gave me a medication containing (unknown to me) codeine, and after three doses I was as high as DeQuincy at his highest. Medication? ugh.

Con amore,
John Joseph

Epilogue

John Joseph died on March 25, 1984 at the age of seventy-three. He and a friend had climbed a hill in back of Lost Thyme from the top of which was a spectacular view. Suddenly, John Joseph exclaimed, "Catch me, I'm falling." He was dead by the time he had hit the ground. On the same day I had written him from London to tell him the sixth volume of the Lyttelton-Hart-Davis Letters had been published and a copy was on its way to him.

John Joseph could have been describing himself when he wrote about George Lyttelton: "Old George is a gem: such a benign and tolerant and sagacious wit." And again: "Can anyone equal Lyttelton's instinct for humaneness: and he was only a teacher!" John Joseph was "only a teacher" but what a teacher!

I am continually surprised at the extent to which he still pervades my life. Shared memories, books, pictures, recipes, wines and architectural enthusiasms make for a potent bond with which death cannot interfere. So much of what I enjoy I enjoy more for having known John Joseph, and I am constantly wishing that he could share my enjoyment, whether it be the latest volume of Letters by Virginia Woolf, or an early novel by Iris Murdoch, or the movie of The Shooting Party, or an article by Robertson Davies, or a Piranesi drawing at an art show.

The other day I was reading an article from a Provence newspaper called L'Aioli in which someone was described as "furfuracious" meaning flaky, and the article went on to say that the word comes from the Latin "furfur" meaning dandruff. I could imagine John Joseph trying to cap that one and thought I must write to him as he would enjoy it. Then I remembered that I couldn't.

In June of 1985, I went to Yorkshire on an architectural tour and finally saw Hawksmoor's Mausoleum at Castle Howard. Knowing I was going to see it, I had with me a small bottle of cognac. I waited until the others had started walking back and then I poured the cognac on the gate of the Mausoleum and murmured "Ave atque vale." I think J.J. would have been pleased.

Appendix

In January 1987 I sent to Rupert Hart-Davis copies of John Joseph's letters in which he mentioned the Lyttelton-Hart-Davis Letters, writing that I thought he might like to read about the great pleasure that John Joseph had gotten from the Letters, and I wondered if he remembered writing the letter which had so mystified J.J. I got a charming letter back from Hart-Davis, enclosing the letter that J.J. had written to him.

THE OLD RECTORY

MARSKE-IN-SWALEDALE

RICHMOND

Patrizia Cara (There is clearly no other way of addressing you, and Carissima would perhaps be somewhat forward),

Very many thanks for your letter and for sending me copies of those delightful letters (may I keep them?). I enclose J.J.'s letter to me which he had forgotten writing. Please let me have it back.

Your address rings many bells, since I was born at 79 Victoria Road, opposite the church, in 1907. If you can find a copy of my book *The Arms of Time* (John Saumarez-Smitooh can surely find you one) you'll read a little about it.

Yours fraternally,
Rupert Hart-Davis

SHELBOURNE, MASSACHUSETTS

22 JULY 1983

My dear Rupert Hart-Davis,

From a remote wild valley in the Berkshire Hills, I write at last to thank you for the five volumes of your and George Lyttelton's letters. This morning I was awake at 5:30 and reread the Vol. IV Swaledale letters to George, with such gratitude as I am too puny to describe. In a madly putrefying world it is good to reach out and find two persons civilised, witty, charming, warm, and magnanimous. What would George say of these foul days of 1983? Acerbic his comment, no doubt, but shining with sagacity.

Thank you for allowing me to number among my friends Ruth, Comfort, Pamela, your children and all those great persons whom you saw (fortunate you) on a day-to-day basis. Thank you, particularly, for your portrait of T.S. Eliot, whom, when I was doing Classics at Harvard, I met at a Classical Club meeting, ages ago of course, the year he held the C.E. Norton Fellowship at Harvard. As for the divine Peggy Ashcroft, I first saw her in Manhattan in *High Tor* with Burgess Meredith, and saw her recently in the film *Sunday, Bloody Sunday*. You have by the deities been steeply blessed, for the persons whose paths you crossed invariably were made of vastly superior stuff. I envy you your friendship with Peter Fleming and his wife (R.I.P.): I still recall the thrill I acquired from Fleming's *Brazilian Adventure* and I still have his essays from his *Rhinoceros* collection.

Forgive my verbosity. But I am copiously grateful.

Believe me to be, sir, always yours sincerely and admiringly,

John F. Joseph